Issues in Contemporary Journalism Education and Practice in Nigeria

Volume 1

Nosa Owens-Ibie

Caleb University, Imota, Lagos

and

Eric Msughter Aondover

Caleb University, Imota, Lagos

Series in Critical Media Studies

VERNON PRESS

www.vernonpress.com

In the Americas:
Vernon Press
1000 N West Street, Suite 1200,
Wilmington, Delaware 19801
United States

In the rest of the world:
Vernon Press
C/Sancti Espiritu 17,
Malaga, 29006
Spain

Series in Critical Media Studies

Library of Congress Control Number: 2025935064

ISBN: 979-8-8819-0329-9
Also available: 979-8-8819-0283-4 [Hardback]; 979-8-8819-0327-5 [PDF, E-Book]

Cover design by Vernon Press. Background image by Anna Tolipova on Freepik.

This book is dedicated to communication scholars and professionals in Nigeria, and the diaspora.

Contents

Foreword

The ever-increasing-sophistication of the media and communication landscape has created an intense desire for the National Universities Commission (NUC) to recently announce the unbundling of the traditional Mass Communication degree programme in universities in Nigeria to eight disciplines in Communication and Media Studies (Journalism, and Media Studies, Information, and Media Studies, Advertising, Public, Relations, Development Communication, Broadcasting, Strategic Communication, Film and Multimedia Studies). This development, coupled with the enormous growth in the media industry in Nigeria in terms of the number of media organisations and adoption of best global practices and technologies, has created the need for new and more specialised instructional and reading materials relevant for use by stakeholders in tertiary educational system in Nigeria. In this context, *Issues in Contemporary Journalism Education, and Practice in Nigeria* is a book designed to not just fill the gap in instructional materials for the new disciplines but a contribution to Communication and Media studies scholarship and practice that touches on the relevant contemporary issues in journalism.

The dynamism in journalism in the digital age demands nothing short of good-quality books that elucidate, and illustrate the emerging or evolving concepts, and principles for better comprehension of theories, and methods by students, scholars and practitioners. This book provides a widely useful compilation in this regard, and in terms of objectives, principles and concepts on issues in journalism education.

The book is indeed timely, especially in respect of the unbundling of Mass Communication in Nigeria. Overall, the book offers students, practitioners and scholars a concrete, useful, and in-depth look at topical issues in Journalism. Clearly written and well organised.

I congratulate the authors and wish them greater energy to do more for the strengthening of the body of knowledge in the area. I hope that students pursuing their undergraduate and postgraduate courses in Journalism and Media Studies, as well as communication scholars/practitioners, will greatly benefit from the contents of this book, and thus, the motive of the book will be achieved. I invite you to get a copy of this book for yourself and get another copy for someone. It should be in every school's professional library.

Professor Joseph Wilson
HOD of Mass Communication,
Federal University, Kashere, Gombe State, Nigeria.

Preface

Journalism in the digital age has taken a different dimension both in theoretical, and practical application. The trends and dynamics accelerated by technology in the industry have created ways for new approaches to better journalistic practice. Today, technology-rich societies are consolidating their alignment with the demands of the digital age, and media industries are grappling with new opportunities which call for fresh insight into issues in contemporary journalism education in Nigeria. The need to expose students to content that will sufficiently prepare them for global challenges is fundamental in this era of digital journalism.

In traditional journalistic writing, news must only be found, verified, and skilfully reported via established mass communication media. The advent of online platforms for doing journalistic business has brought about a transformation in the conventional news production chain. There are phenomenal changes in the ways global citizens communicate and interact. The era is one in which the mass media industries are highly disrupted. With mediatisation, digitalisation, and audience participation in the public sphere, old theories, concepts, curricula, and pedagogy of communication and media studies are increasingly put to the test.

This book, therefore, focuses on diverse issues, including the utilisation of the digital space for economic and national development, social activism and political participation, the spread of fake news and hate speech, security challenges, public relations, media consumption, and mediated experiences.

Issues in Contemporary Journalism Education, and Practice in Nigeria employs a wide range of theoretical and methodological approaches to address contemporary issues, to provide students, professionals, and scholars critical perspectives in journalistic engagements. The way society consumes news, and content and the pedagogical context of issues in journalism have changed dramatically.

Current issues in journalism education are presented in ten Chapters. Chapter One examined the mass media, classification and types of mass media, historical development of the print media in Nigeria, electronic media discourse, the internet, the internet in Nigeria, social media in Nigeria, types of social media, uses of social media in Nigeria, challenges of social media, characteristics of the internet, and social media, factors that influence the development of mass media in Nigeria, and the combat press of the Nigerian civil war, and boom in government, and private press.

Perspectives on journalism and Nigerian women, factors that determine news selection in journalism, other elements that affect news selection, the basic principles of journalism, gendered journalism, and factors fuelling gender discrimination in Nigerian news media, common hindrances encountered by Nigerian women journalists were the focus of Chapter Two. Issues addressed in Chapter Three include Nigerian media, and the watchdog role, as well as watchdog journalism in broadcast media.

Chapter Four covers the topics of investigative journalism, its purposes, the characteristics of an investigative reporter, the distinction between conventional and investigative journalism, obstacles facing investigative journalism, its prospects, and how to get started. Chapter Five focuses on political journalism and reporting, political news reporting, components of excellent political reporting, political news reporting in Nigeria, and political reporting principles.

The topics covered in Chapter Six include citizen journalism, the opinions of academics on it, its global emergence, its advantages and disadvantages in Nigeria, and its implications for mainstream media. Chapter Seven covers peace journalism and conflict management; the principles, the ten commandments, the emergence of peace journalism, its characteristics, its five guiding principles; the practice of peace journalism in Nigeria; its challenges; journalists as conflict perpetrators; the post-conflict peacebuilding process; conventional strategies for reporting conflict; lessons from American versus Chinese approaches to conflict resolution; and media, and conflict reporting in Nigeria.

Chapter Eight examines conflict reporting in journalism, perspectives on conflict, phases of conflicts, triangles and levels of conflict analysis, conflict and manifest conflict reporting, and latent conflict reporting: and the Niger-Delta crisis. Chapter Nine explores artificial intelligence and algorithmic journalism, its advantages and disadvantages, challenges, and potential future implementation of algorithmic technology in journalism practice. While global journalistic threats, mapping threats to journalists in the world, and protection, and mitigation strategies to the threats are the focus of Chapter Ten. Chapter Eleven is the summary chapter that highlights the main issues discussed in all the previous chapters.

The authors could be contacted through. nosa.owens-ibie@calebuniversity. edu.ng, eric.aondover@calebuniversity.edu.ng or nosowens@gmail.com, aondover7@gmail.com.

Acknowledgements

Praise and honour to God Almighty for providing the ability, insight, discernment, fortitude, and grace necessary to complete this book. The authors are also grateful to the numerous scholars whose works have been cited in this book. We are indebted to Professor Joseph Wilson, Head, Department of Mass Communication, Federal University, Kashere, Gombe State, for reviewing the manuscript and writing the foreword.

About the Authors

Nosa Owens-Ibie, PhD, University of Ibadan (1992), is a Professor of Communication, Media and Development, and former Vice-Chancellor, Caleb University, Imota, Lagos, Nigeria. He earned his B.Sc. (Honours) and M.Sc. degrees in Mass Communication from the University of Lagos, in 1980 and 1983. He was the first to be appointed a professor by Caleb University in 2011, became the first substantive Deputy Vice Chancellor of the University in 2018, was variously Head, Department of Mass Communication, Dean of Students, Dean, College of Social and Management Sciences, and Dean, College of Postgraduate Studies. On April 9, 2013, he delivered the maiden inaugural lecture of the University *Communicating an Implosion: Signs and Wander, Popular Culture and the Crumbling of Empire*. He coordinated the establishment in 2013 of the Association of Communication Scholars & Professionals of Nigeria and was the General Secretary until 2024. He has authored and co-authored academic and professional articles in Nigeria and other parts of the world. He was a columnist in *The Guardian on Sunday* and *Sunday Punch* newspapers for a decade and scripted for programmes on television and radio. A panellist for over two decades for Diamond Awards for Media Excellence (DAME) in Nigeria, he has consulted for International development agencies including WHO, UNICEF, UNFPA, and IOM, facilitated trainings and other capacity building programmes for government agencies, multinational companies and non-governmental organisations, and coordinated the development of toolkits for ActionAid Nigeria in the areas of Health and Women's Right. His coordination activities in ACSPN includes several collaborations with UNESCO, including on the production of the Media and Information Literacy Non-Curricular Activities Materials for Sierra Leone, four of which have now been adopted globally by UNESCO, and available on the UNESCO website UNESDOC Digital Library. A former Federal Government of Nigeria postgraduate Scholarship beneficiary, he is a Fellow of the International Institute of Journalism, Berlin, Germany and Salzburg Seminar, Austria. He is a member of the Nigerian Institute of Public Relations, Associate Member, Advertising Registration Council of Nigeria (ARCON), and member of both the Nigerian Academy of Letters and International Association and the International Association of Media and Communication Research (IAMCR).

Eric Msughter Aondover, Ph.D, is a lecturer in the Department of Mass Communication at Caleb University, Imota, Lagos. Aondover is a communication scholar and has published papers in several national and international scholarly journals and attended and participated in several conferences and workshops on communication, media, and journalism. He is a member and National Students Coordinator, Association of Communication Scholars & Professionals of Nigeria (ACSPN) as well as a member of the African Council for Communication Education (ACCE), the Association of Media and Communication Researchers of Nigeria (AMCRON) and a Fellow of Social Science Research Council (FSSRC), USA, and an Award Winner of Campus Journalism as "Syndicated Writer", 2018 and "Book Author", 2019. Aondover serves as the Editor of MedDocs Publishers LLC, USA, Guest Editor of Science Publishing Group (PG), New York, USA, and Editor of UNISIA Journal as well as Sparkly Research Journal.

He is the author of the following textbooks: Foundations of Communication and Media Studies (2024), Media Narratives on Hate Speech in Nigeria (2023), New Approach to Mass Media Writing (2022), Fundamentals of Media English (2022), Media Law and Ethics in Nigeria: Issues, Principles and Practices (2021), Contemporary Approach to Social Science Research (2020), A Prescriptive Approach to Development Communication (2020), Fundamentals of Mass Media and Communication Research (2018), Selected Themes in Specialised Reporting (2018), A Prescriptive Approach of Peace Journalism and Development (2018), Understanding Safety and Protection in Nigeria's Journalism (2017), The Ghost Gun (2015), Tears of Destiny (2012) and many more.

Chapter One
Historical Antecedent of Mass Media in Nigeria

Human beings have always found ways to communicate with one another and make sense of their existence because, like air and food, communication is essential to human survival. Traditional African societies were distinguished by various forms of communication, including town criers, drums, gongs, and festivities, which served the communication needs of the time and continue to do so today. Modernisation has transformed society into a mass society where people live in dispersed geographic locations and share a variety of cultures. Communication has, therefore, changed significantly from interpersonal to mass communication. Mass communication is a mode of communication in which messages are transmitted to a large, scattered, and heterogeneous audience through a variety of channels known as the mass media (Maweu, 2017). The possibility of mass communication, therefore, depends on mass media. It is therefore important to understand the history, growth, and development of media of mass communication, especially in Nigeria.

This chapter x-rays the evolution of the mass media in Nigeria, and discusses the specific factors that contributed to the growth and development of the mass media in the country. The mass media industry in Nigeria is vibrant, characterised by various stakeholders and forms of media. The media in the country have continued to grow since they came on board from pre-colonial, colonial, and post-colonial periods.

Within the socio-political, economic, cultural, and historical framework of society, the mass media functions as a social institution. These dynamic elements impact the mass media's structure and personality. When Siebert and his colleagues noted in their seminal four theories of the press that "the press always takes on the form, and coloration of the social, and political structures within which it operates", they made this historical reality abundantly evident. In particular, it mirrors the social control system (Siebert, et al., in Chiakaan et al., p. 1956 2023). Though the modern Nigeria media was a creation of colonialism, and the Christian mission, it has developed within the changing historical circumstances of the country. As Oso noted, "The Nigerian mass media system has developed within the dynamics of the country's political economy" (Oso in Odunlami, p.10, 2023). It reflects the character of Nigerian politics and society and the uneven structure of socio-economic development.

The Mass Media

The mass media (plural) or mass medium (singular) is also known as mass communication media. The term has been explained by many scholars. Dominick (2005) defines mass media as the channels that are used for mass communication. Hassan (2013) concurs that mass media are the vehicles of mass communication. Ciboh (2006) defines the term mass media as devices for moving messages across distance or time to accomplish mass communication. According to him, "machines that serve as paths, ways, or means for doubling, repeating, or representing communication that would otherwise be limited to two persons or a group of persons in a face-to-face setting" (Ciboh, 2006, p. 2). Chiakaan et al., (2023) posit that mass media are agents of mass communication since they are the ones that carry messages or ideas or information to members of the public. The message from the above definitions clearly implies that mass media are the various channels that facilitate the dissemination of information from senders (media organisations) to diverse audiences in different settings.

However, what makes mass media is not just the technological devices that media organisations such as radio and television broadcasting houses use but also the experts in the organisations, the policies, and their management (Asemah, 2011). Mass media provide information, education, and enlightenment to the public or members of society (Musandu, 2018). The government also depends on the mass media to reach members of the public, and the public equally depends on the mass media to reach the government (Lippmann, 2017). Mass media stimulate trade or businesses, mobilise the public toward particular goals, and play a key role in sustaining democracy. The fact is that any organisation that desires to deliver its messages to a wider audience at different locations needs the media of mass communication (McQuail, 2010).

Classification and Types of Mass Media

Different types of mass media exist. The twenty-first century's widespread use of digital communication makes it difficult to categorise them because of arguments over whether or not to include gadgets like computers, video games, and cell phones in the category of mass media. However, mass media are typically divided into two categories: print media and electronic media. Radio and television are two of the main components of electronic media, but there are other forms such as movies or videos, audio recordings, and even emerging media like the internet and its different components, like social media. One distinctive characteristic of electronic media is that, in order to operate, each of the aforementioned categories of electronic media needs electricity or a power source. For instance, radio, television, cinema, and even the internet requires some form of electric power before they can function. The major strength of electronic media is the fact that they have the capacity to reach a wider audience, and they, especially radio and television, break the literacy barrier. People who cannot read or write can access information from electronic media, especially radio and television. However, electronic media have several weaknesses that undermine their growth in Nigeria.

The main disadvantage of electronic media is that the average Nigerian finds it challenging to access messages due to its financial consequences. For instance, a TV and radio, a digital device such as a laptop or smartphone, and an active internet connection are required in order to obtain information from electronic media. Public viewing places are few and far between, and many Nigerians cannot afford these gadgets due to poverty and inadequate infrastructure. Nigeria's inadequate power supply is another issue that reduces the efficacy of electronic media; as a result, many households and viewers miss important information, education, and entertainment even when they air, because there is no power supply and no generator or solar energy available because of financial difficulties. There is also the problem of poor internet access (Wilson et al., 2023).

The second classification of mass media is the print media. This is arguably the oldest mass media in history. It encompasses newspapers, magazines, books, posters, leaflets, and the like. Okunna and Omenugha (2013) assert that print media have saturated the world due to several advantages they possess over electronic media. Okunna and Omenugha further state that the major advantage of the print media is the fact that the audience can review and revisit/read the messages received through the print media at any given time. This also implies that a reader can access the messages even when he or she is not around when the message was first made available to the public. This contrasts with traditional television and TV shows, which are frequently ephemeral and difficult for viewers to re-watch unless they are rerun. The main issue with print media, though, is that in order for the public to access the content, they must possess a certain degree of literacy. This suggests that in order to comprehend messages found in books, periodicals, newspapers, and other media, one must be able to read. These days, social media platforms like Facebook, Instagram, WhatsApp, and Twitter augment these traditional media. Mass communication has been transformed by these platforms; practically everyone may now produce, receive, and share information at any time and from any location.

Despite the challenges associated with both the print and electronic media in Nigeria, the mass media have continued to proliferate the Nigerian society. Today there are several radio, and television houses in Nigeria. Most of these media stations belong to the government, and few belong to private individuals and organisations, especially religious organisations. In the same vein, the print media, especially the newspaper industry in Nigeria, is said to be one of the most vibrant in the continent of Africa. Several newspaper and magazine organisations are in existence. Both print and electronic media in Nigeria have a rich history.

Historical Development of the Print Media in Nigeria

In Nigeria and throughout the world, print media is perhaps the oldest mass media. Numerous narratives have been presented concerning the history of print media. As an example, Nwabueze (2011) has argued that the origins of print media may be traced back to Europe in the fifteenth century, when a number of publishing houses were established to produce theological texts utilised in the movement for church reformation. Okunna, and Omenugha (2013) reveal that print media started in China in 500 A.D. However, scholars unanimously acknowledged the fact that though newspaper gains more popularity and attention in the discourse about the history of the print media, books preceded the emergence of newspapers. There is no doubt missionaries and colonialists came to the shores of Nigeria with several books and other related print materials. Media historians in Nigeria, however, believed that the development of print media in Nigeria started in 1846 with the establishment of a printing press in Calabar by Rev. Hope Waddel, a Presbyterian Missionary. Waddel's publications were Christian religious pamphlets and books (Akinkuotu, 1999).

However, in 1854, Reverend Henry Townsend established another printing press at Abeokuta, and on 18th November 1859, Rev. Townsend published what is said to be the first newspaper in Nigeria. The paper was called *Iwe Irohin fun awon Egba ati* Yoruba. It started as Yoruba language fortnightly but became bilingual in 1860 when an English language supplement was added (Omu, 1978, p. 7). The main objective of Townsend in establishing the paper was "to get the people to read i.e to beget the habit of seeking information by reading" (Hyde in Omu, 1978, p. 7). This was, of course, in addition to its ecumenical and proselytising mission. However, records show that *Iwe Irohin's* main impact was in local politics. According to the pioneer historian of the Nigerian press, Fred Omu, the paper was Townsend's "chief weapon in his ambitious political propaganda and shrewd manoeuvring for power in Egba land". He employed the paper in his involvement in Egba-Lagos politics to the extent that the Lagos colonial administration lodged a complaint against him to the colonial office (Omu, 1978, p7&8). The paper died because of its involvement in politics. It should also be noted that the *Iwe Irohin* was part of the instruments of British colonialism and mercantilist interest. It was used to promote the so-called legitimate trade. This point in the history of *Iwe Irohin* is very important in the sense that it signalled the instrumentalist's political character of the Nigerian press. This is to say that politics has been a major factor in the development and growth of the media in Nigeria right from the beginning, and it has been a chief weapon in the struggle for power by politicians in the country (Arregui & Cheruiyot, 2023).

This fact is quite evident in the development of the newspapers that came after the *Iwe Iroyin* in Lagos during the colonial period. After the *Iwe Irohin*, Lagos became, and still remains, the centre of the newspaper business in Nigeria. The first newspaper was the *Lagos Times* and *Gold Coast Colony Advertiser*, which came on the newsstand on Nov 10, 1880. It was founded by Richard Beale Blaize of Yoruba, and Sierra Leonian origin. This was followed by the *Anglo-African* 1863-1865, owned by Robert Campbell. Other newspapers that followed include the *Lagos Observer*, established by J. Blackall Benjamin, the *Eagle, and Lagos Critic*, the *Lagos Weekly Times* (May 1896). One of the most notable newspapers of the period was the *Lagos Weekly Record*, owned by John Payne Jackson. The newspaper lasted only for eight years (Bender, 2000).

It went out of circulation in October 1867 during a political crisis called Ifole, which led to the expulsion of the Europeans from Abeokuta. As colonial rule became more entrenched in Nigeria, and with the merging of *Lagos Colony* and the Southern Protectorate in 1861, many newspapers came on board. These included the *Nigerian Pioneer*, 1914-1937 by Kitoye Ajasa, *The African Messenger* by Ernes Sisei Ikoli 1921-1926, and *Daily Times*, which was established in 1926 by a group of business persons among several other newspapers of the time. Some of the newspapers were pro-colonial establishments, others were commercially driven, and others claimed to be neutral but without taking any form of antagonism against the colonial masters. Many of them took on the colonial establishment head-on. We must note the main factors that motivated the establishment of these colonial Lagos presses. First was the emergence of an educated elite, made up of mostly freed slaves from Sierra Leone. Some of the journalists/ proprietors have been trained as printers by the missionaries. These pioneers also claimed that they were motivated by the desire of enlightening and educating their countrymen as well as championing their causes (Omu, 1978, p. 28).

However, there were other underlying motives and reasons. Omu advanced two of such reasons. The first among these newspapermen were "those conscious to recover from financial ruin arising from bankruptcy of European firms". Second, "those in want of employment owing to dismissal, and resignations from jobs, prohibitions from legal practice amid incapacitation by illness" (Omu, ibid). There is no doubt that these are strong economic reasons. But later, and as the realities of colonialism unfolded the political factor gained prominence. The nationalists took over. The press was used by the nationalist politicians as a veritable instrument in their agitation against the colonial establishment. This reinforced the political instrumentalisation of the Nigerian press. Omu observed that the early press was inevitably a political press (Omu, ibid, p.11). Two British scholars have also noted this historical point: Nigerian journalism was thus created by anti-colonial protests, baptised in the water of nationalist propaganda, and matured in party politics. The separation of politics and journalism has remained incomplete, and the allegiances to professional and political goals have created conflicts whose resolution in daily practices underpins much of contemporary Nigerian journalism (Idowu, 1999).

However, by 1937 a class of fearless and nationalistic newspapers emerged. Prominent among this class of newspapers was *The West Africa Pilot* Group of Newspapers by Dr. Nnamdi Azikiwe, a core nationalist who employed his paper as a weapon in the fight for Nigeria's independence. Close to the independence, several other newspapers also emerged, such as *The Nigerian Tribune, The Lagos Daily News, The Daily Service, The Daily Telegraph, Gaskiya Tafi Kwabo,* among others. These papers were owned by politicians and political parties of the time. After independence and up to today, there have been several newspapers, and magazines that have come on board in Nigeria, some of these include *National Concord, Newswatch, Tell, Tempo, The News, The Punch, Thisday, Leadership, The Nation, The Vanguard, The Sun, The Guardian* among others. These print media have continued to evolve, serving the information needs of Nigerians and the global community. It was believed at a stage that the Nigerian print media industry was the fastest growing in the continent of Africa (Okunna & Omenugha, 2013). That may still be the case, although the global trend in the shrinking space of print media development has also reflected in the Nigerian media.

Electronic Media Discourse

The electronic media in this chapter is limited to radio, television, internet, and the social media:

Radio: Radio is the earliest form of electronic mass media, several inventors contributed to what it has become today. Key among these scientists and inventors are Heinrich Hertz, who, in 1887, produced the first radio waves. Another significant contributor to the invention of the radio is Gugliemo Marconi, who, in 1895 invented the wireless telegraph used to send voiceless signals across the Atlantic Ocean (Esan, 2023). However, it was in 1906 that the actual transmission of voice was made possible by Lee De Forest, who made what heralded the arrival of the modern radio (Okunna & Omenugha, 2013). In Nigeria, the history of radio can be traced to colonialism. In 1932, the colonial masters established the British Empire Service to relay BBC programmes from England to the colonies including the current Nigeria (Esan, 2023). Later, in 1936 Radio Distribution Service was established in Lagos to distribute the programmes of BBC. The distribution centres had a studio in Lagos, which helped to step down BBC's programmes to special radio boxes paid for by subscribers. Radio Distribution service grew rapidly as similar stations were established in different parts of Nigeria, namely Abeokuta, Calabar, Enugu, Ibadan, Ijebu Ode, Kaduna, Kano, Port Harcourt, and Zaria. In 1951, the Nigeria Broadcasting Services (NBS) was established, and some Radio distribution centres were converted into full-fledged radio stations.

As Nigeria gained independence, every region established its radio station while the Federal Government was in control of the NBS station. This trajectory continued with the creation of more states. In 1966, after the coup that ended the first Republic, the military government abolished the regional system of government and created states. The new states established their stations, and by 1978, when the military returned power to civilians, the Federal Government established the Federal Radio Corporation of Nigeria (FRCN), also known as Radio Nigeria. FRCN became the umbrella for all Federal Government owned stations providing content for national audiences, while the Voice of Nigeria (VON) primarily served the international community (Bortolotto, 2024).

In 1992, the Federal Government deregulated the broadcast industry, leading to the establishment of many private radio stations, especially Frequency Modulation (FM). Another form of radio broadcasting is community radio broadcasting, common in many academic institutions in Nigeria. Aside from these radio stations serving as platforms for learning in communication departments and faculties, they serve the academic communities and their environs by providing news and entertainment among others (Freedom of Information Act, 2011).

Television: The history of television globally shows that the medium emerged in the 1920s, Vladimir Zworykin, a Russian-American, was credited with the major idea that led to the invention of modern TV as a mass medium. Television broadcasting started in Nigeria in 1959. It was established by the Government of the Western Region led by Chief Obafemi Awolowo in Ibadan. The Television station was known as the Western Nigerian Television (WNTV). The success of WNTV in promoting the government of Awolowo was the catalyst for the establishment by other regional leaders of their television stations. This started with the Eastern Nigeria Television in Enugu in 1961 and Radio-Television Kaduna in 1962. In the same 1962, the Federal Government also established the Nigeria Television Service. Subsequently, when the regional system of government was abolished, all the regional stations were converted to the current Nigerian Television Authority (NTA), while the new states established their own stations. Currently, each state in Nigeria owns a Television station, while the Federal Government's NTA has at least a subsidiary in every state (Chiakaan, 2020). Like radio, in 1993, the Federal Government deregulated the television industry, hence, many private stations emerged. The earliest private stations that came on board were Minaj TV, and African Independent Television (AIT). Others that later emerged and became so popular today include Channels TV, Television Continental (TVC), Silverbird TV, Arise TV, and News Central TV.

The Internet

The internet is a worldwide communication system that links multiple separate networks together so that two or more computers on a network can exchange information. Global communication and data access are made possible by this globally interconnected network system, which consists of several government, private, official, public, corporate, and academic networks. Internet evolved in 1969, under the Advanced Research Projects Agency Network (ARPANET) project, to connect computers at different universities and the U.S. Defence Department. Subsequently, engineers, scientists, students, and researchers started using the network for exchanging information and messages. No single individual, company, organisation, or government owns or runs the internet. It is a globally distributed network made up of interconnected autonomous networks, however, there are few institutions that have a bit of control (Wilson et al., 2023). They include:

a) The Internet Governance Forum (IGF) steered by the United Nations (UN). It is a multi stakeholder platform that encourages conversation around policy, and the issues related to Internet governance.

b) The Internet Research Task Force (IRTF): creates long term research groups/ working group that promotes research related to internet protocols, applications, architecture, and technology.

c) The Internet Architecture Board (IAB) oversees the technical and engineering development of the Internet by the Internet Society (ISOC).

d) Internet Corporation for Assigned Names, and Numbers (ICANN) through its Internet Assigned Numbers Authority (or IANA) manage the allocation of Internet Protocol addresses (IP), and the domain name system (DNS). It maintains the repository of internet standards by distributing internet numbers to regions for internet use and ensure universal protocols.

e) Internet Engineering Task Force (IETF). It develops and promotes a wide range of Internet standards dealing with standards set by the Internet protocol suite.

f) International Organization for Standardization (ISO 3166). It outlines Internet standards.

g)   World Wide Web Consortium (WSC): creates standards enabling an open platform for all.

h)   The Nigerian Communications Commission (NCC), as a regulator, oversees the activities of all Internet access and Services providers. Pursuant to this objective, the Commission designs programmes, and initiatives, organises events, and carries out research on Internet Governance developments.

i)   The Nigerian Internet Governance Forum (NIGF): It is a multi-stakeholder forum on internet and digital policy issues (DSIM Team, 2020; TechTarget,n.d; NCC n.d)

Today, communication is greatly aided by the Internet. It facilitates the exchange of messages via text (mail, chat), images, video, and audio, all of which are now commonly used in everyday activities, including online shopping, virtual workspaces, online education, and interpersonal communication. Consequently, a vast amount of information is carried and transferred between devices via the internet, a global network of computers, and other electronic devices. To achieve various communication goals, devices such as laptops, desktop computers, GPS units, smartphones, vehicle alarms, and video gaming consoles are linked to the internet. Every computer on internet is identified by a unique IP address. IP Address is a unique set of numbers or label (E.g.110.22.33.115) which identifies a computer location (Heaton, 2024).

The Internet in Nigeria

Internet use in Nigeria began in the middle of the 1990s. The National Centre for Communication Technologies was the nation's first internet service provider (ISP) when it was first established in 1991 although few people, and organisations then had access to the internet. As a result of the need for reserved Internet access, Nigerian Telecommunications Ltd (NITEL), Interswitch, and vee networks were developed (Adomi, 2005). Governmental organisations, academic institutions, and other entities were able to offer internet services to their diverse clientele in 1996 when the Nigerian Communication Commission (NCC) granted licenses to internet service providers. In the early 2000, access to the internet expanded speedily with the advent of General Packet Radio Service (GPRS)wireless networks, and the emergence of mobile phones with generation networks such as edge 2G, 3G, 4G. The advancement in the production of computer systems from desktop to laptop and palmtop, contributed to the development of the internet (Gaitano et al., 2022). The internet offers enormous opportunities to execute a lot of tasks - and almost instantly, with anyone in any part of the world. Some of these activities are: communicating via email, connecting in a variety of ways, and building communities online, Chat, and instant messaging, and other everyday uses (including finding information online media. Online shopping, bills payment, streaming).

Social Media in Nigeria

Social media is a type of communication that takes place on the internet. Users can create web content, share information, and engage in conversations on social media networks. These days, social media use and human routine are strongly related. But that wasn't the case with human routine 25 years ago, particularly in Nigeria (Aondover & Pate, 2021). The idea of social media was born out of the development of information and communication technology. When Facebook, Twitter, Myspace, and other social media platforms gained popularity and were made available via desktop computers and the internet in the early 2000s, social media adoption started gaining ascendancy in Nigeria. Human contact is being shaped technology and keeps evolving. Alson, and Misagal (2016) posit that social media, and smart phones are inextricably connected because, smartphones have the features of computer system which enable users to interact regardless of space, time, and geographical boundaries.

Types of Social Media

1. The six major types of social media include:

2. Social networks: Social Network sites are online platforms that allow users to create a public profile and interact with other users. Examples are YouTube, WhatsApp, Instagram, TikTok, Tumblr, Twitter, and Pinterest.

3. Bookmark Sites: Social Bookmarking sites are sites that allow users to store bookmarks on a cloud-based server, which users can access from anywhere

4. Social news: Social news sites provide ways to promote content in a way that can attract more traffic. E.g. Digg, Reddit, and Delicious.

5. Media sharing site: Sites that enable users to store, and share their multimedia files (photos, videos, music) with other users. E.g. Instagram, YouTube.

6. Microblogging sites: Sites that allow instant messaging and content production. Short messages are shared with an online audience to improve engagement. E.g. Twitter, Tumblr, Pinterest, Instagram.

7. Online forum sites: are sites dedicated to conversation, usually through posting questions, answers, and responses. Quora, Reddit, GitHub, Imgur (Wilson et al., 2023).

Uses of Social Media in Nigeria

a) Communication: It fosters effective interaction between people or groups of persons.

b) Digital marketing; uses internet platforms for showcasing or marketing products for people to see, and buy.

c) Entertainment: It is used for the promotion of songs and videos.

d) Sharing: Friends and family who are dispersed geographically can connect virtually and share information, documents, and videos.

e) Content creation; It is used for the circulation of user generated content.

Benefits of social media to Nigerians

a) Social media helps in reaching a large number of audiences.

b) Social media provides direct connection with audience.

c) Social media helps in building relationships.

d) Social media increases visibility.

e) Social media facilitates e-learning (Wilson et al., 2023).

Challenges of Social Media

Social media share almost similar challenges with the internet. Some of the challenges are:

I. It can contribute to social isolation.

II. It can be used as a veritable tool for cyberbullying.

III. It is often used for the spread of fake news.

IV. People who often explore social media are likely to compare themselves to others in a way which affects self-esteem.

V. It can increase feelings of depression and anxiety.

Characteristics of Internet and Social Media

a) Global Nature: The internet, and social media are global in nature. Billions of people all over the world are linked through this massive, interconnected web of computer networks and social networking platforms.

b)   Interactivity: The interactive characteristics of the internet, and social media allow users to exchange information between the platforms and users (Technology/human interactivity) or between users of the platform (Human/Human interactivity).

c)   Accessibility, and usability: The internet, and social media are available to everyone who has the necessary devices, and knowledge to use them.

d)   Re-publication: The internet, and social media allow content to be easily re-published or shared on numerous occasions to relevant audiences.

e)   Hyperlinks: The internet is facilitated by the use of hypertext mark-up language (HTML) for the creation of links that enable a user to navigate from one source or related sources by clicking on the link. A click on a link takes the user from web-site to website or to other files within a particular website. The hyperlinks are available on social media platforms, especially using symbols to connect users to other social channels.

f)   Multimedia: The internet, and social media electronically deliver combination of media, such as video, still images, audio, and text in such a way that can be accessed interactively by users.

The internet and social media have become integral part of the everyday life of Nigerians, providing citizens with extensive benefits, and opportunities to empower themselves in different ways (communication, gaming, online banking/transaction, bill payment). However, there are challenges such as increased risk of cyber-bullying: the Internet poses the serious challenge of increased risk of cyber-bullying, Increased Risk of identity, Spam, and unsolicited advertising, spreading fake news, misinformation, disinformation, and mal-information worldwide. Nevertheless, Internet and social media would continue to impact activities globally.

Factors that Influence the Development of Mass Media in Nigeria:

The growth and development of the mass media in Nigeria have been historically influenced by multiple factors. These factors can be grouped into:

Political Factor

Politics is about the struggle for power to lead and control state resources. This struggle requires interaction with the people as well as the ability to persuade the people. Hence, the mass media have become strategic instruments for political power mongers. The media remains one of the first institutions governments try to take hold of because of perceptions about the media's power to influence the people. The growth of mass media around the world, including Nigeria is significantly influenced by several political factors. For instance, radio was introduced by the colonial masters as a tool of political control of the colony (Nigeria) rather than servicing the people. The colonial masters invested in the Radio Distribution Service, and the introduction of Nigerian Broadcasting Services (NBS) continually shaped the behaviuor, and attitude of the people of the colony in their relationship with the colonial masters in a way which affected the agitation for independence. This gives credence to why the Radio Distribution service and its later subsidiaries primarily broadcast BBC contents produced in London (Sambe, 2018).

Political dynamics that contributed to the development of the media in Nigeria did not end with the colonialists. The agitation for independence by nationalists such as Herbert Macaulay, Nnamdi Azikiwe, Obafemi Awolowo, among others, led to the establishment of several media outfits. Another political development of note was the misunderstanding between Governor Macpherson and Chief Obafemi Awolowo. Macpherson used the radio established and controlled by the Colonial authorities to attack and discredit Obafemi Awolowo as an unfaithful and unpatriotic person because he (Awolowo) and his party (Action Group) disagreed with the Macpherson Constitution as well as called for the independence of Nigeria (Aondover, 2019).

Awolowo tried to have access to the State Radio to respond to the allegations against him, but he was denied access. The crisis further showed nationalists such as Awolowo how important electronic media could be in the fight for political survival, hence the agitation for regional governments to be allowed to own electronic media. This was made possible by the Lyttleton Constitution that followed, and by 1959, the Western Nigeria Television was established by the Western Region under Chief Obafemi Awolowo. Awolowo, and his party continued to use WNTV to further their political relevance across the region, and Nigeria. When the leaders of other regions noticed the political power of electronic media, they also invested in it by establishing their stations. Subsequently, Military governments played key roles in the growth and development of mass media. It was the Military that established the FRCN, and the NTA. State governments that later emerged also knew how important the media could be; hence, they established them in their states (Aondover et al., 2022).

State governments continue to invest in radio and television as major tools for government to propagate their policies and achievements, mobilise the public, and ensure required feedback. In furtherance of this logic, politicians in Nigeria maintain active media liaisons with the mass media and journalists to ensure favourable coverage. Some of them have established print media organisations and radio and television stations. Examples are TVC, owned by

Bola Ahmed Tinubu, and Gotel Radio and Television, owned by Alhaji Atiku Abubakar. Even though many of these media outfits claim to be independent of their owners, it is obvious that they promote the political interests of their owners. The important point is that these politicians have, no doubt, contributed to the development of the media in the country. These media outfits owned by politicians are generally well-equipped and have well-trained personnel, with evidence that their staff compensation packages, in some verified instances, are better than what government stations offer.

Economic/Commercial Factor

The mass media are both ideological, political, and economic/commercial organisations. Their development has been greatly influenced by economic and commercial considerations, especially since the 1980s, following the emplacement of neo-liberal economic policies. The response to the demand to gain market share and meet other challenges in the competitive market led to changes in the structure of most organisations and the tweaking of ethical standards and professionalism. The trend of aligning content to meet the demand of the advertisers gained ascendancy. Advertisers provide some subsidy for the media through patronage. It is a case of he who pays the piper, dictates the tune. The media that will survive in the market must be able to produce the right type of content for their audiences (Oso, 2018). For instance, in the Daily Times example, before the Daily Mirror acquired it in 1947, the economic prospects of the country were a major consideration in the calculation of the company. In a memorandum, a director of Daily Mirror involved in the acquisition, wrote:

The prosperity, present, and future of the country was of course of maximum importance to any newspaper enterprise…at that time, the position was good. To my mind the future was full of promise. There was prosperous cool, and team minds. There had at that date I wrote never been a completely adequate survey but the government is starting now…it is hoped there is oil. Altogether, there are big development plans in being…. I was confident about the country, and therefore about a new newspaper prospect (quoted in Echeruo, 1976).

The West African Pilot, whose establishment revolutionised the Nigerian press, especially in the type of stories and presentation style which adopted the mass appeal of the American penny press. According to Coker, "the day-to-day domestic, and human problems of the people were being dramatized for readers, entertainment, and pleasure" (Nwagbara et al., 2018). A Nigerian historian, Biobaku, also noted that "the era of mass appeal has come" (Biobaku, nd, p. viii), the style paid off in circulation and revenue, which facilitated the establishment of other newspapers in different parts of the country by Azikiwe.

Other newspapers like The Daily Times had to re-package themselves to compete.

The large capital required to establish a media organisation has, however, created a huge entry barrier to those who may be interested. This has meant that, in the main, the ownership and control of the media has remained by the few businessmen – politicians with the capital. The influence of big businessmen and powerful political actors on the survival of the media is evident in the demise of Next newspaper, established by the Nigerian one-time Pulitzer winner Dele Olojede, and the Citizen, the news magazine based in Kaduna (Okon, 2021). The leading news magazines which flourished between the 1980s, and 1990s - Newswatch, The News, and Tell either became defunct or lost their prime positions due to a mix of factors, including economic considerations.

During the Shehu Shagari administration many broadcasting organisations including the NTA, and FRCN encountered problems. Budget funding from the government had dwindled due to the economic crisis of the period. Many stations commercialised the coverage news, and airtime was sold to state-owned organisations who sponsored weekly promotional documentaries, and independent broadcasters, including comedians. Cheap programmes were imported from various sources, including soap operas from the U.S., and Latin America. Entertainment has taken over the neglect of public service programmes, which now come mainly in the form of studio-based interviews and discussion programs, and more often than not, promote controversies rather than enlightenment and civic engagement. These all targeted the audience (Omoera, 2023). The privatisation and commercialisation of broadcasting in the country was also a response to the downturn in the economy during the Ibrahim Babangida military regime, which introduced the Structural Adjustment Programme (SAP), and other neo-liberal economic policies. Many private radio and TV organisations are driven more by the logic of profit-making than professionalism and a public service philosophy.

It should also be noted that the urban focus of the Nigerian media is due mainly to economic, and commercial considerations. The urban centres in Nigeria are the centres of economic activities, the location of the big advertisers, the elite, and even the educated youth. From a critical political economy perspective, Murdock and Golding have rightly argued that:

> the interplay between the symbolic, and economic dimensions of public communication…. how different ways of financing, and traceable consequences for the range of discourses, representation, and communicative resources in the public domain, and for the

organisation of audiences across, and use (Murdock & Golding, 2005, p. 60).

The Mass media, while seeking to inform, educate, and entertain the public, also seeks economic sustainability and profitability. The economics of mass media has become an important issue that has also influenced the growth of the mass media in Nigeria. Many national dailies in Nigeria today are owned by business people, some of whom are active politicians. Similarly, some leading electronic media like Channels TV, and Arise TV are owned by private investors.

The involvement of these investors in the media industry has a lot of implications for the media, including the quality of the equipment Some of these organisations have reporters across the states of Nigeria, and across nations of the world. This development has given the Nigeria media visibility around the world and strengthened their operations. The structure of the country's development has also influenced the development of the media. It is evident that Lagos and the South West as epi-centres of economic activities in Nigeriahas a concentration of the media in the country. The country's ethnic and religious pluralism has influenced the development of the media, their structure, and consumption patterns. The southwestern media has been labelled as Ngbati press, the South East, Ndigbo press, and the Niger Delta press. This ownership, management, and recruitment tend to reflect the ethnic configurations (Peter, 2014).

Technological Factor

Technology has been the backbone of mass media since inception. Every phase in the development of mass media was determined by a given technology. From Johann Gutenberg's invention of the printing press in the fifteenth century, to the current computer or internet age, technology has kept evolving, influencing the growth, and development of the mass communication field (Rodny-Gumede, 2015).

Although technology has helped the Nigeria media to enhance the quality of content as well as the scope of coverage, technology, particularly the internet, has helped the Nigerian media to converge. Many Nigerian print media organisations have both online, and offline versions, with electronic media also combining terrestrial services with online platforms. The online helps them to provide content in multi-media forms. Several traditional newspapers provide video and audio contents thereby increasing their audiences, and revenue. Technology has led to the emergence of major online media outlets in Nigeria. One such media outlet is the *Premium Times*, established by Dapo

Olorunyomi, a veteran of adversarial journalism, who has grown the medium to be a national and regional journalistic force.

Another key influence of technology on the Nigeria mass media is the development in Satellite broadcasting. Local radio, and television stations in Nigeria are now accessible anywhere around the world because they have been digitalised, and hosted by satellite service providers such as DSTV, and Star Times. That global advantage has also resulted in improvements in the contents, and increase in their airtime (Sackey et al., 2022).

Legal Factor

The mass media do not exist in a vacuum but within a social milieu guided by laws and regulations. The existence and operation of media in any society are regulated by the laws of that society. This understanding is an indication that there are legal dynamics that have shaped the growth, and development of media in Nigeria. Legal factors determine media ownership, and operations (Sani, 2017).

Constitutional provisions and several laws ended the monopoly of media ownership by the government at the centre. This was first seen in the Lyttleton's Constitution of 1954, which gave regional governments the right to own electronic media. That encouraged the Government of the Western Region of Nigeria to establish a television station even before independence, a development that also motivated other regions to do same, hence, leading to more electronic media outlets in the country. The 1993 decree deregulating broadcasting also enabled the emergence of more private stations in the country. However, the growth of Nigerian media over the years has been undermined by the high licensing and renewal fees charged by the National Broadcasting Commission (NBC). Many media outlets are struggling to survive due to poor revenue generation. Many prospective media owners could not meet the legal, and financial requirements to start transmission (Tafida, 2015). Similarly, there are cases of fines, and legal clashes between media organisations, and the regulatory body (NBC). All these legal tussles have contributed to shaping the development of the mass media in the country.

Religious Factor

Religion had been part of what is now generally referred to as Nigeria's culture even before the coming of Christianity and Islam. However, Christianity, and Islam made religion more pronounced because of the efforts of the adherents of the two religions in propagating their beliefs. The mass media have been central to the propagation of the two religions. In fact, the development of mass media in Nigeria cannot be discussed without mentioning the role of religion, especially the Christian religion. According to Obidiegwu in Tafida (2015) the Christian religion introduced the conventional media in Nigeria. It is on record that Christian missionaries long before colonialism brought printed materials such as books, and pamphlets to propagate the Christian faith. The first printing press was established by a Christian missionary in Calabar. The first newspaper (Iwe Iroyin) was established in 1859 by a Christian cleric, Reverend Henry Townsend, a British missionary under the Church Missionary Society (CMS). The paper (Iwe Iroyin) is highly celebrated in the journalism world because it preceded the establishment of other newspapers in Nigeria (Sambe, 2018).

Religion has continued to influence the development of the mass media in Nigeria. Today, there are several religious media outlets, especially television stations in Nigeria, broadcasting via Satellite to audiences around the world. Examples of TV Channels owned by Christian groups or churches in Nigeria are Love World by Christ Embassy Church, Dunamis TV by Dunamis International Gospel Centre, Dove TV by The Redeemed Christian Church of God (RCCG), Celebration TV of Omega Fire Ministry, COZA TV of Commonwealth of Zion Assembly. Examples of TV channels owned by Islamic groups are Sunnah TV, IQRAA, and Islam Channel. Religious media outlets majorly focus on propagating religion but there is no doubt that they have made a mark in the development of the mass media in Nigeria (Udomisor, 2013).

Socio-Cultural Factor

Culture is always a topical issue in any society because culture defines people, their uniqueness, and the entirety of their existence. In a multicultural society like Nigeria, cultural survival and supremacy are serious issues. Though it has been established that the mass media shape and preserve cultures, it is also expedient to note that socio-cultural forces influence the growth and development of mass media in Nigeria. For instance, several groups or communities establish TV stations to preserve their identities and promote their ideals. An example is the Bwatiye TV of the Bachama people of Adamawa State.

Another social-cultural factor that has contributed to media growth in Nigeria is the changing taste or expectation of media content by consumers, especially the youth. It is evident that youth in Nigeria majorly desire entertainment content. This development has given birth to TV stations dedicated to entertainment and reality shows that have enhanced the revenue profile of some television stations. Similarly, the growing football culture or sports followership is contributing to the growth of mass media (Uwugiaren et al., 2020). There is a dedicated sports radio called Brila FM with stations in Lagos, Abuja, Onitsha, and Port-Harcourt. There are print media that are specialized in sports coverage. NTA sports, and TVC Entertainment are some channels with significant sports and entertainment programming.

The Combat Press of the Nigerian Civil War

There were vibrant private newspapers, and government-owned press at the onset of the civil war in Nigeria. The private press included newspapers like the *West African Pilot, Nigerian Tribune, Eastern Nigerian Guardian,* and *Daily Times.* Government newspapers included the *Daily Sketch, Nigerian Observer, Nigerian Outlook* which later became *Biafran Sun, Biafra Spotlight,* and the *New Nigerian* (Yékú, 2022).

In the north, the Nigerian Citizen, which was established in 1948, metamorphosed into the New Nigerian newspaper on January 1, 1966, barely 14 days before the first military coup. Established by the Northern Regional Government, the newspaper had the objective of defending the Northern region, and projecting its views on all matters in the national political struggles. The New Nigerian maintained a non-partisan stance while the crisis was simmering but projected what it believed was good for the nation in the throes of political convulsion. The newspaper thereafter demonstrated outright partisanship by supporting the Federal Government (Sambe, 2018).

On the Biafran side, the Eastern Nigeria Spotlight was established in December 1966 and published by the Government of Eastern Nigeria. The newspaper had both English and French supplements for Nigerian and overseas readers. When the Republic of Biafra was proclaimed on May 30, 1967, the newspaper, in its June 1, 1967 edition, announced a change in name to *Biafra Spotlight.* There was also the Biafra Sun that metamorphosed from the former *Nigerian Outlook* at the outbreak of the civil war. Besides these Biafran newspapers, there were others like the *Daily Flash,* the Star, *International Daily News,* Daily Standard, and the Leopard. These were mainly the propaganda machinery of the Biafran government. The newspapers were sometimes produced in notebook sizes and on improvised exercise books, ostensibly due to a lack of newsprint for production during the war. *The Renaissance* was established by the Ukpabi Asika regime in the liberated part of the then East Central State during the war for effective governance of the newly liberated state. It continued circulation and lasted till after the end of the war. On both the federal and the rebel sides, the newspapers of the Civil War period were actively involved in the politics of the war (Chiakaan et al., 2023).

Boom in Government and Private Press

The end of the first republic saw the termination of party ownership and funding of newspapers. Government-funded newspapers became the vogue.

The 1970s presented Nigeria with a good opportunity for growth and development. The macroeconomic indices as a result of the oil boom was conducive to progress in the various sectors of the economy. This boom in the economy positively impacted the newspaper business. The increase in the number of states following the Civil War encouraged the proliferation of government-owned newspapers. The old Mid-West State pioneered the state ownership of newspapers during the Nigerian civil war when it established the Nigerian Observer on May 30, 1968. The East Central State's Renaissance was also established during the war while the Western State inherited the Daily Sketch from the old Western Region. Kwara State launched the Nigerian Herald in 1973. Other newspapers in this category were the Nigerian Chronicle in the South-Eastern State, Daily Star in the East Central State, Nigerian Tide in Rivers State, Nigerian Standard in Benue Plateau, and *The Triumph* in Kano State (Chiakaan et al., 2023).

The return to civilian rule under the Second Republic of President Shehu Shagari (1979 1983) led to the explosion of the privately owned press. Although The Punch newspaper came up with a visually more aggressive style in 1973, with front-page pin-ups and satirical cartoons, which resonated with the Lagos public, the 1980s witnessed the emergence of powerful groups, which were financed by ambitious executives for whom a press company represented a way of increasing their influence. In 1980, the *National Concord* newspaper was set up by billionaire M. K. O. Abiola, and in 1983, *The Guardian* was established by Alex Ibru. In 1984, Sam Amuka-Pemu launched the daily *Vanguard.* In 1987, Musa Yar Adua established The *Reporter* in Kaduna (Oso, 2018).

One significant factor about these newspapers was the availability of trained and skilled labour to undertake the task of informing, educating, and entertaining the people. Individual businessmen, rather than the government, established these newspapers. Some of them are discussed here:

Concord: The Concord group of newspapers, based in Ikeja, Lagos, was established in 1980 by business mogul and politician Chief Moshood Abiola. The first title published by the stable was the National Concord, published along with its weekly edition, *Sunday Concord,* on 1st March 1980. A few years later, he added three vernacular newspapers to its stable in Nigeria's three languages. The newspapers were *Isokan* (in Yoruba), *Udoka* (in Igbo), and *Amana* (in Hausa). The Concord group later added four more publications to its stable: *Business Concord, Weekend Concord, African Science Monitor,* and *African Concord.* Later, the Concord group set up newspapers in various parts of Nigeria known as *Community Concord.* Known for its fearlessness and attack on political opponents, the National Concord, played a key role in supporting the National Party of Nigeria (NPN) against Chief Obafemi Awolowo's Unity Party of Nigeria (UPN) in the Second Republic politics (Oso, 2018).

Guardian: *The Guardian* newspaper is one of the outstanding newspapers in Nigeria. It was established on the 27th of February, 1983 by Alex Ibru from Delta State. Among those who weaned the paper at the cradle stage were Dr. Dele Cole, Dr Stanley Macebuh, and Lade Bonuola who were all former executives of the Daily Times (Nwabueze, 2016).

Post Express: *The Post Express* newspaper was owned by Chief Sony Odogwu, a top businessman. The founding management team comprised Dr Stanley Macebuh, Dr Fred Onyabor, and Obaro Ikime. The motto of the paper was "Justice in Service of Community". It promised accurate and fair reports, as well as reasoned and informed comments. The management's first news papering revolutionary step was the simultaneous printing of the Post Express in Lagos and Port Harcourt (Odunlami, 2023).

Daily Trust: The Weekly Trust was first published on March 21, 1998, by Alhaji Kabiru Yusuf, a former Senior Lecturer in the Department of Political Science at Usman Dan Fodio University, Sokoto. It later went daily with the name *Daily Trust*. The Daily Trust was the first daily newspaper to be published in the Federal Capital Territory, Abuja, in January 2001. Media Trust Limited, Abuja prints and publishes the Daily Trust and Weekly Trust (Oso, 2018).

The Sun: The Sun newspaper, which began publication in 2003, is published in Lagos by Chief Orji Uzor Kalu, former Governor of Abia State. Its style of page design makes it unique among other Nigerian newspapers. The Sun is known for its distinct method of reporting news events and its fearlessness. It made a mark through its detailed reporting of the Tsunami disaster of December 26, 2004. The Sun's courageous and consistent reporting of the celebrated removal of former Inspector General of Police, Mr. Tafa Balogun, as well as the dramatic and controversial "resignation" of Chief Audu Ogbeh as chairman of the then ruling party, the PDP. was believed to have contributed to increasing the readership of the newspaper.

The establishment, expansion, and development of the media in Nigeria can, therefore, be attributed to a number of factors. These include sociocultural, religious, technological, political, and economic aspects. Although the history of the media has been fraught with difficulties, it is undeniable that it is a journey that may never end, given how society is constantly changing and how the media, by their very nature, are prone to these changes (Chiakaan et al., 2023).

Chapter Two
Perspectives on Journalism and Nigerian Women

Journalism evokes the image of reporting on or writing about significant stories or events having social relevance. Since not all writing falls under the category of journalistic writing or reporting, there are basic rules for choosing news in journalism. When all the requirements are met, a plot like this can be chosen for publication as a news piece. The activities of acquiring, analysing, producing, and presenting news and information are all part of journalism (Tilak & Vidyapeeth, 2020). It is, in essence, the result of these endeavours. There are specific characteristics and practices that set journalism apart from other endeavours. These elements set journalism apart and give it significance and relevance in democratic societies, as more news and information tend to circulate in societies that adhere to democratic principles.

According to Asemah and Ekerikevwe (2013), journalism is a communication style that depends on asking and answering the following questions: Who? What? Where? When? Why? How? The phrase "who" now refers to the individuals, persons, or people who are the cause or the effect of an event when we expand the scope of these questions. For example, the people who lost their lives in a traffic accident are the "who" in the incident. What happened is the subject of the story, and that is the query "what" addresses. "When" in journalism refers to the date and occasionally, the exact moment an event happened. Electronic media worries about time because of the perception of immediacy, whereas print media is primarily concerned with dates. The question "why" sheds light on the cause or conditions of the event. For instance, the Federal Government has received a $10 billion donation from the World Bank to help fight the nation's high rate of insurgency. The "how" describes how the event happened.

Journalism requires a lot of thought, intellect, and work. This is because not all occurrences or events are appropriate for reporting by journalists. It is the timely reporting of an occurrence that is important to the vast majority of society. The people who engage in this activity are known as journalists. The practice of journalism encompasses more than just publicly visible events. Sometimes a given occurrence needs to be explained so that the average person may grasp it. Other times, thorough inquiries into specific events are required to determine their causes or the secrets behind them. Since they all fall under the umbrella of journalism, this implies that journalistic writings can have a variety of formats. Regardless of the format, society learns about the incident through a communication channel that reaches a vast audience that is widely distributed and anonymous. Journalism's objective is to continuously change society and re-establish its core values by supplying it with information on a regular basis (Aondover & Pate, 2021).

A day without news information poses a serious threat to society's survival because of how valuable media is to it. This is because journalism contributes to highlighting key elements of a democratic society, including an informed populace, freedom to participate in decision-making, and accountability to the people by those who exercise power on their behalf.

To put it another way, journalism provides people with the knowledge they require in order to make wise judgments about their own lives. When the press delivers the necessary information, citizens can take part in the government process. A strong media culture is a prerequisite for the accountability that citizens can expect of their government and that government must provide. Strong journalism informs society about people's cultural life, social amusement, and places to unwind, among other realms of human endeavour. It alerts the business community to changes in stock market prices, the rate of inflation, governmental monetary policies, foreign reserves, the purchasing power of wages, and the outlook for the country's youth (Mojaye & Aondover, 2022).

Certain tasks carried out by the journalist are important for society's efficient operation. These include, among others, the gathering, and dissemination of information about happenings both inside and outside the society is referred to as the information function. To instruct: This role describes the reporter's capacity to create messages intended to impart knowledge, alter behaviour, and clarify processes. To entertain: Communications released or broadcast with the goal of calming listeners and reducing their stress. These tasks are carried out by the reporter's inventiveness as they search for newsworthy events and those that go untold. According to Aondover et al. (2022) a reporter engages in these activities when he or she visits press conferences, catastrophe or accident scenes, protests, and other events that are newsworthy.

The position of the reporter in journalism is vital. He is the one who documents and summarizes the daily activities. However, it must be made clear that no reporter in contemporary journalism is able to cover every issue of interest. Each journalist focuses on a certain subject or what is called 'specialised reporting'. He or she frequently covers the beat, developing expertise in the coverage of beat-related issues.

Factors that Determine News Selection in Journalism

The obvious issue that arises here is: Why are some stories chosen over others? What requirements have been met by these stories to be considered reports? The standards are known as news value in journalism. According to Ekhareafo et al. (2016, pp. 6-12), they are:

    I. Timeliness

    II. Prominence

    III. Oddity

    IV. Conflict

    V. Proximity

    VI. Consequence

    VII. Human interest

    VIII. Magnitude

Timeliness: This speaks of the moment that an event took place. According to Moemeka (1991), the length of time between an event's occurrence and the news dissemination is a key consideration when choosing which stories to publish. The quality of timeliness increases with decreasing time differences. A four-month-old event has already become stale. It has been surpassed by other events. The audience enjoys an event's currency. Because of technology, timelines now greatly influence the value of news, which is why many media sites report stories as they happen. There is one exception to this rule: the significance of the time component diminishes if an event has significant repercussions.

Prominence: It is the importance attached to a story or the personality involved in a story. Personalities are at the centre of the news; they tell followers stories through their words and deeds. The saying "There is God o!" - credited to Patience Jonathan, the former first lady and wife of Goodluck Jonathan, will stick in the minds of many Nigerians. In reality, the phrase "there is God" is used frequently to remind people that they are not in charge of life and that God is not powerless. Unfortunately, when she said this in the midst of the Chibok girls' abduction story, it sparked a heated debate on social media and other media outlet. Is it true that many Nigerians are not familiar with the saying? Why was the statement the subject of so much interest? According to Aondover et al. (2022) news is largely built around the lives of personalities.

Oddity: Strangeness or novelties are terms used to describe this news value. It alludes to things that cause people to wonder, such as "eeeh", "nawa", and "wonders will never stop". Therefore, all events that raise questions are considered odd, especially if they are perceived to be unusual. Strange stories include that of a man sleeping with his mother, a lady giving birth at the age of 65, and a woman getting pregnant and giving birth to a monkey.

Conflict: They are those disputes, tensions, and crises that affect a group, society, and even the political system. In the world, for example, the current war between Russia and Ukraine, the storming of the Congress by the supporters of Donald Trump during the January 6, 2021, Capitol Hill uprising on the presidential result. Conflicts tend to excite public interest. That is why the Boko Haram insurgency and kidnapping cases in Nigeria frequently make the headlines.

Proximity: We often feel cut off from what is going on in other regions of the world. This is a result of their being distant from our environment. Therefore, proximity describes the distance that an event or series of events has from a media audience. For this reason, a great deal of happenings in other parts of the world could go unnoticed by the media. An event gains significance from its closeness to the public.

There are three parameters to look at proximity: time, space, and the psychological.

a) Proximity of time: it refers to the time frame of an occurrence or how recent an event occurred. For instance, there can be anxiety over a fire outbreak on a nearby street because of worry that if nothing is done to put it out, it might spread to the neighbourhood. The freshness, and immediacy of an event to the people are therefore related to the proximity of time.

b) Proximity of space: This is also known as spatial closeness. It is the geographic separation between the news source and the audience. Anyone living in in Lagos would normally be concerned if there is a riot in a particular area of the city.

c) Psychological proximity: It is the sentimental value assigned to an upcoming event. During the xenophobic attacks in South Africa in February 2015, many Nigerians instinctively reacted, sensing that it would affect a large number of Nigerians residing in that country. Many families were forced to ask their loved ones to leave the area of the country during the height of the Boko Haram conflict due to the recurring headlines of deaths. Knowing that there are vaccinations available to treat HIV/AIDS offers those who are infected with the disease hope for appropriate medical attention. Despite the fact that the discovery may be distant, the news has the potential to instil hope in patients and the public.

Consequence: It is the most likely effect an incident will have on society. For example, due to Nigeria's largely monoproduct economy, there was a great deal of interest when militants in the Niger Delta started fighting for resource control. Due to the disruption of oil industry activities, yes, there was a dislocation of the economy, and government at various levels had challenges meeting their obligation. The effects of an incident on society are always of interest to newsmakers. As a result, problems like strikes, gasoline price increases, and wars impacted the economy with fallouts like inflation, job loss, and insecurity.

Human interest: This refers to how deeply an event affects people's emotions. Human interest refers to the kinds of stories that arouse sympathy, rage, fear, hope, disappointment, and joy. Of note was the story of a pregnant woman who was among the people that were kidnapped during the Abuja-Kaduna train attack by bandits in 2022, who gave birth in captivity. It generated considerable interest from the public.

Stories with a human interest inspire feelings of identification. The level of human interest determines whether something is newsworthy. The typical response to a human interest story may include crying, feeling sad, smiling, dancing, and shouting.

Magnitude: It speaks to the scope or magnitude of an occurrence. There is a tendent to want to know who was involved, how much harm was done, and how much it will cost when something happens. It is also the magnitude of the occasion. For instance, the most common query after an accident is "Hope there is no death?" How many, if any? What levels of injuries were there, and is the vehicle repairable?

Other Elements that Affect News Selection

Other factors or elements have a role in news selection. Gatekeepers see them as having value for news as well. They are referred to as small conventional news values as outlined by Ufuophu-Biri (2006):

IX. The audience factors;

X. Discretion of the journalist;

XI. Availability of news;

XII. Ownership influence;

XIII. Commercial/advertisers influence;

XIV. Influence of technology; and

XV. Economic factor.

The Basic Principles of Journalism

Journalism does not flourish on assumptions. The practice is governed by concepts that have evolved over time. Researchers refer to them by a number of names, such as the theory of journalism, ethnic values, and journalism canons. The principles are.

1. *Truth:* What is known to be true is what is supported by facts and integrity. The truth must always be told in all journalistic work. It involves making conscious attempts to gather information for a journalistic piece that uses specific facts and numbers to support the argument. Such facts should come from trustworthy sources that can be independently checked. Such reporting needs to be accurate when citing facts to support an article. Asemah and Ekerikevwe (2013, p. 6) did an excellent job of capturing the essence of truth as a principle. They stated that telling the truth fosters trust between the public and the media and shows respect for people.

2. *Public interest:* The Nigerian Constitution notes that "the press, radio, television, and other agencies of the mass media shall at all times be free to uphold the fundamental objective contained in this chapter, and uphold the responsibility, and accountability of the government to the people" in Chapter II, Section 22, of the 1999 Constitution as amended. The journalistic standard should be this clause. Despite the fact that there are a variety of things that can impair a writer's judgment, their dedication to the public interest ought to always come first (Ekhareafo et al., 2016). The general public has a right to knowledge and a right to be heard. The commercialization of media is a developing trend in the media industry. Nonetheless, the majority of media proprietors should strike the right balance between economic, and public interests.

3. *Independence:* This principle's fundamental tenet is that practitioners shouldn't publicly promote themselves. The ability of the professional to remain objective during an incident. It is the capacity to remain composed and resist being influenced by particular allegiances and divisions. While maintaining contact with sources is ethical, this relationship must not jeopardise the public's right to fair, and accurate reporting. A practitioner's ability to perform his duties to the public will be influenced by his perception of himself as society's gatekeeper.

4. *Objectivity:* This is extremely near to the independence principle. It means to report without bias. In other words, it refers to the writer's capacity to set aside personal biases in favour of what a case or piece of fiction's evidence suggests. A witness's description of an incident that includes multiple perspectives rather than just one. A one-sided view or attitude to an issue is prevented through the contribution of various witnesses during interrogation. When faced with a situation

that requires a diverse viewpoint, it is important to make an effort to examine a variety of facts, and viewpoints in order to achieve a balance. Objectivity is, therefore, measured by the level of competence, relevance, truthfulness, and dynamism of a reporter.

5. *Significance and Relevance:* There is an enormous amount of information being exchanged. Because of this, not every story may be assumed to be of public interest. Therefore, the emphasis should be placed on information that is of considerable value to citizens, according to the principle of importance. Ohaja (2005) pointed out that the author must respond to inquiries like, "How good is this event? Is it a historic occasion or merely business as usual? Is it an important or lofty issue? Is the incident or problem local, national, or global? What response is expected from the reader? Will he be able to ignore it?"

6. *Comprehensiveness and Proportionality:* The inclusion of all societal segments in news coverage is the fundamental purpose of the concept of comprehensiveness. Media outlets do this by dividing their news coverage into national, and local news. Many people refer to it as community, metro-file, or rural reports. The idea supports pursuing a broad-based journalism while emphasizing important events. On the other hand, proportionality promotes maintaining key stories in the right perspective without ignoring them. Media organisations may have a propensity to focus on comprehensiveness while ignoring the crucial details.

7. *Personal conscience:* The right of a journalist to express their opinions on a subject is at the centre of the concept of personal conscience. Everyone must not always think along the same lines. An individual's personal conscience empowers him or her to stand up for ideals they firmly believe to be true. A journalist can object to his editor's slant on the news. The concept of conscience encourages ethical behaviour without sacrificing one's morals for material benefit.

8. *Transparency or attribution:* Conflicts of interest could occasionally arise for a reporter. He might be obligated to report on a conflict between two communities even though he is a member of one of them, like in the case of a war. The requirement is that a reporter be honest and transparent about his or her personal interests, which could skew their reporting, and that they own up to or reveal them.

9. *Attribution:* It simply means citing your informational source(s). The reporter is protected from plagiarism by it. Some journalists frequently conceal the source of their material by using anonymous sources. Journalists must identify their information sources unless doing so could hurt the source. This would lessen the amount of "beer

parlour" journalism that has replaced traditional journalism in Nigeria.

10. *Sensitivity:* When covering a live event or serving as a commentator for a broadcast media outlet, you are not obliged to report severe incidents like a fire outbreak, stadium collapse, or a fight. The reason is to reduce the potential negative consequences that such reporting might have on viewers and listeners.

    Aside from live events, you should always use compassionate language in interviews, especially with grieving and traumatized families. The journalist must show compassion regardless of what the bereaved chooses to say.

11. *Ethics versus laws:* Ethics and law are closely related because they both work to improve society and promote responsible citizenship. Every civilisation has rules that serve as guidelines for its citizens, including journalists. However, a journalist's desire for a better society may push him or her to conduct information search that are illegal. If the information revealed would benefit the public, it is ethical in journalism.

12. *Forum for public criticisms:* In journalism, this is referred to as the right of reply. People have the right to respond to any allegations or criticism made against them in the media. Media companies work hard to implement this idea. The idea also enables people access to the media so they can write letters to the editor or emails to a particular programme producer to say what they think about what is going on in society. The media are in a privileged position, and act as socializers due to the channel offered for citizens to convey news. The ability to think critically, which is required to change society, becomes possible when the media influence arguments.

Consequently, the production and distribution of a report on the ways in which facts, ideas, people, and events combine to create the "news of the day" and, to some extent, inform society is journalism. It deals with the task of promptly creating or narrating captivating stories about social developments. As a result, there exist various kinds of journalism, each influenced by a particular social development or interest.

1. Development Journalism: Protests against the way wealthy countries reported about third-world countries were the starting point for this. New World Information and Communication Order (NWICO) and New International Economic Order (NIEO) were proposed by leaders of developing countries in order to facilitate the free flow of information.

Development journalism primarily focuses on acquiring, analysing, and disseminating news and information about development through a variety of outlets that are relevant to people. Development journalism is described by Soola (2003) as a pragmatic, skilled, dialectal, composite, and purposeful practice that involves reporting on socially acceptable programs and projects that aim to improve people's quality of life. In addition to speaking and writing in the local tongue and covering subjects like the environment, health, agriculture, population growth, food security, housing, and human rights, it must facilitate a two-way information flow between the rural and urban economies.

2. *Precision Journalism*: Journalism practices need to evolve in the information-rich world of today from the basic news report to a more in-depth, meticulously researched piece with societal ramifications. Precision journalism, according to Ukonu (2005), is a novel kind of reporting in which adept communicators use social research methods to gather, analyse, and persuasively present data to their intended audience. According to him, it offers concise and convincing facts in an environment that makes them intelligible and beneficial. Simply put, information is backed up by verifiable facts and real data. Precision journalism includes the use of experiments, surveys (opinion rolls), statistical methods, and content analysis. Its objective is to use quantitative methods to make events, characteristics, behaviours, or attitudes into members that can be analysed.

3. *Civic Journalism*: In the late 1980s, and early 1990s, the concept of civic journalism initially became popular (Tilak & Vidyapeeth 2020). Through engagement and discussion of national issues, it seeks to enhance the quality of civic life. Civic journalism assists citizens in a nation where there is apathy toward the political process in order to become active participants in the political process who can engage the government on how to best run or improve society while fulfilling their civic responsibilities by paying taxes and engaging in the political processes that are typical in a democratic society.

Lack of civic involvement, manipulation in democratic processes (such as Russia's meddling in the 2016 US election), and even hackable electronic voting systems (e-voting) are all contributing factors to the general decline of democracy. In this context, civic journalism proponents noted that if democracy is to regain its foothold and grandeur in the modern world, the media must be more receptive to public feedback and take the initiative to engage the people.

Thus, journalism is the process of obtaining, disseminating, and publishing news and opinions about society through the media. Questions like "Who", "What", "Where", "When", "Why", and "How" are asked and then answered in journalism. Journalists inform the public about society and disclose information that would otherwise be secret. Journalists also provide information, analysis, and elaboration on subjects that are pre-public (Tijani-Adenle, 2019).

Nigerian journalism in the middle of the nineteenth century was largely practised by amateurs who used their journals to either confront the colonial authorities or spread a cause and a belief. Early in the 1960s, Nigeria witnessed the further evolution of journalism practice. At that time, there were only two universities offering journalism studies: the University of Nigeria, Nsukka, which began operations in 1961, and the University of Lagos, which was founded in 1962, while its mass communication programme commenced in 1966. By completing mass communication, and journalism courses, students could graduate from these two universities with a certificate in mass communication. According to Emenyeonu (1991), prospective students were first hesitant to major in journalism because the most popular professions at the time were architecture, engineering, law, and medicine. However, today, this has changed as a result of the transformation in journalism in the twenty-first century and because of the sophistication in technology. Journalism in Nigeria today has continued to grow in line with global trends.

Currently, there are increasing indications of a growing passion for the study of mass communication, as seen in the exponential growth in the number of applicants (mainly young women). Making the field appealing to many Nigerians. Has this changed? When did this change? Why did it change? (Pusapati, 2024). Since the 1960s, when journalism was first offered as a specialty course in mass communication the majority of students were female. However, it is on record that few of these students decide to pursue a profession in journalism following graduation. Patricia et al. (2015, p. 5) highlight the dearth of female reporters in the Nigerian media as a clear and urgent problem that existed in the past and still exists now. The number of women journalists in the industry is relatively small when compared to the number of graduates from journalism-focused programmes at Nigerian universities. This would need to change to reflect the needs of inclusivity and the growth of the profession and industry.

From historians who chronicled the lives of the early pioneers to cultural studies experts who developed theories on how women use social media, academics from a variety of disciplines have examined the status of women in journalism (Tijani-Adenle, 2019). The gender gap in newsrooms has also been measured by sociologists and communication scientists, who have discovered that stereotypes are reinforced by the media (Pusapati, 2024). Numerous studies have discovered that many people enrol in journalism programmes as a course of study rather than as a means of employment (Patricia et al., 2015). This suggests that, in higher education, women like taking communication courses but do not want to get into the field professionally (Pusapati, 2024).

This might be the consequence of fear, discrimination, how people view women journalists, or even a husband's decision to be hired as a journalist.

Gendered Journalism and Factors Fuelling Gender Discrimination in Nigerian News Media

Despite the diversity of professional skills, the ultimate goal of journalism is to sufficiently inform the target audience about local, thematic concerns. Journalism not only informs the public about important facts, and events, but it also provides a forum for competing viewpoints, safeguards government, institutions, and the public, advocates for change that is in the public interest, and constantly seeks the truth. Whatever their career path, a good journalist needs to be able to write well, handle a heavy workload under pressure, have a variety of skills, have job experience, and above all, have a nose for news (Ekeli & Enobakhare, 2013).

The extent to which media organisations are gendered has been demonstrated by communication experts such as (Anyanwu, 2001 & Akinfeleye, 2011). This suggests that gender norms are common in this field of work. In newsrooms, the idea of what a journalist does, regardless of gender, is deeply embedded on many levels. The dynamics, development, and organisation of Nigerian journalistic groups are impacted by gender segregation. First, several scholars note that the media organisation has a sizable and horizontal sex divide. Women are notably underrepresented in fields like journalism and media, which are known for their high levels of authority and prominence (Mesmer & Miller, 2024).

According to Ratcliffe (2020), the culture and atmosphere of the Nigerian news media sector exposes female journalists to sexism, sexual harassment, and other forms of abuse, as well as dangerous settings and gender-based discrimination. Other journalists and media management personnel recognise the existence of gender-based abuses and discriminations and seek to control them, whereas some media organisations disregard them and expect journalists to defend themselves against such discrimination, as well as from unsafe working conditions in the newsroom.

This notion is also reflected in the culture of journalism. An organisation's unwritten rules specify the duties and responsibilities of its labour force (De-Clercq, 2002). The cornerstone of these norms is the shared values, symbols, and ideas that employers embrace, whether consciously or unconsciously, and which have a substantial influence on their behaviour. Social norms and professional career standards still reflect these cultural beliefs, which are often taken for granted. They create connections, behaviours, and an internal "gendered sub-structure" in the company. For a long time, men have controlled the journalism field. There are several reasons why female journalists choose not to work in the field (Van Dalen, 2012). Nonetheless, many choose attractive jobs in public relations, advertising, radio, and television to print journalism-related jobs like reporting (Mesmer & Miller, 2024).

Many societies are thought to be biased against women obtaining an education due to traditional cultural views (Ali, 2010). According to him, among the many reasons that might have led men to be more prominent over female journalists in Nigeria's media industry and, consequently, not present a positive image of women in society, is the unwillingness of women to practice journalism. Men in the community also believe that women may lose their sense of value and dignity as women if they are subjected to the cruelty of the profession, especially in the Nigerian context of journalism practice. As a result, many female journalists in media organisations usually show a lack of excitement for their work, which lets their male competitors outperform them at work and in the office (Okunna, 2005).

The pressure to marry and start a family or to select any other job path that allows them adequate time to raise children responsibly might also discourage young women from pursuing a career in journalism. There is also the issue of gender bias in the way people view women who work in journalism or use information technology; many of them believe that these women are incapable of using reason or taking organised action. If girls are permitted to work with men, they will completely forget real or imagined limitations and develop an interest in pursuing a career as a journalist. Women need to highlight their important roles as moms and housekeepers in professions like journalism. Meanwhile, women and men can work in the profession of journalism (Okunna, 2005).

The findings of Okunna (2005, p. 15) indicate that newsmakers and reporters of both sexes are more evident in the media in relation to topical issues, news, and those who report it. Okunna goes on, "Gender relations in Nigeria are characterised by a notable imbalance that is harmful to women". He contends that tradition, society, religion, and other elements have contributed to the continuous widening of the gender gap in Nigeria by keeping women in a submissive role.

Common Hindrances Encountered by Nigerian Women Journalists

1. *Social and Cultural Norms Constraints*

Many of the obstacles female journalists experience in furthering their professional relevance are fundamentally gender-related (Okunna, 2005). In Nigeria, there is a great deal of imbalance in gender relations that works against women. Tradition, culture, religion, and other factors have all contributed to the gap between men and women in Nigeria, with women still in positions of disadvantage. Female journalists tended to be given less demanding beats or specialisations. According to Ali (2015, p. 41), "the female gender is seen as biologically unfit to carry out the tasks that come with being a journalist". For example, female journalists historically had fewer opportunities in traditionally "masculine" fields such as political analysis, sports journalism, and photojournalism. But this is beginning to change.

Another challenge is the cultural expectation of responsibilities that women are expected to perform. Unlike their male colleagues, women were seen and treated as not having the time to handle the demands of a media career. Women's traditional roles in caring for children, household chores, and meal preparation, especially in Africa, tended to limit their capacity to devote the same amount of time to job requirements as their male counterparts, especially in the absence of support mechanisms. Consequently, women's underrepresentation in journalism is partly due to their marital duties, which affects their availability. Regretfully, as noted by Palm and Marimbe (2018), only a small portion of female journalists go on to assume senior managerial positions.

2. Vertical Gender Discrimination in Journalism

The hierarchical allocation of positions is another example of how gender has permeated the structure of the journalism industry. Although more women are employed as journalists now, they still do not hold decision-making authority (Tijani-Adenle, 2019). Significantly fewer women than men hold such positions in journalism with substantial symbolic and power capital. Even in countries where there is gender parity in employment, women who can rise to higher positions in journalism are still uncommon.

According to Unaegbu (2017), women in journalism thus face "the glass ceiling", an imperceptible barrier that hinders their advancement. The underrepresentation of women at the highest levels of media organisations is a result of several interrelated factors. First, female journalists are often excluded from the informal sharing of professional knowledge and socialisation. Second, there is a discrepancy in the possibilities that male and female journalists have for on-the-job training (Chocarro, 2019). This disparity can be linked to the idea that because female journalists may be less stable in employment and leave organisations or choose to work part-time, media companies investing in women's training may not receive a guaranteed return on their investment (Ali & Hassoun, 2019).

3. *Horizontal Gender Discrimination in Journalism*

There is a gender divide in the news and media sectors, and there is a horizontal division in the journalism industry (North, 2016). In conventional "softer" female news domains and low-status media sectors, including human interest, lifestyle, and news, there is an overrepresentation of female journalists. However, when it comes to controversial news issues like politics, business, and crime, men outnumber women. According to some analysts, the societal division between the public and private domains is reflected in the gendered differentiation between serious and light news.

Since women are typically confined to the home, they participate more in the positive news rhythms that align with their household responsibilities. On the other hand, significant news beats which are linked to the public domain and press censorship in democracies are customarily dominated by men. Many journalists assume that journalism is gender-neutral, therefore, even if these distinctions are evident, they refuse to acknowledge the gendered nature of news issues. The number of women working in journalism is correlated with the respectability of the media landscape. Compared to more well-known media sectors, women journalists have more access to less well-known media sectors. Using the broadcast business as an example, women's presence has grown despite the medium's declining prominence. However, Tijani-Adenle (2019) references the velvet ghetto theory, which contends that a fall in status and compensation will occur as more women join the media as journalists.

Chapter Three
Watchdog Journalism in Nigeria Broadcast Media

The media is an essential democratic institution. It is an important organisation that supports liberty, restrains the government's power, and works to enhance society (Shardow & Asare, 2016). There is broad consensus among media professionals and scholars regarding some of the vital roles that the media plays in democracies. These include establishing a platform for discussion and a diversity of opinions, agitating, swaying public opinion, and acting as a watchdog over the powerful and rich by informing the public about matters of governance, exposing corruption, and stopping wrongdoing. The media protects and monitors the public by acting as a watchdog.

Because of its inherent advantages over print media, broadcast media, in particular, can reach a larger audience through news and other programmes. These advantages include the ability to reach a larger audience simultaneously and its low mental demand, which appeals to all viewers (Ojomo, 2009). Because of these inherent qualities, broadcast media have a greater responsibility to advance the development agenda and, most importantly, to monitor and protect the public from the excesses and abuses of public authorities, of which Nigeria's broadcast media are passive.

The media in Nigeria has received praise for playing an essential and prominent part in the fight for independence as a watchdog. It is also widely praised for its tenacity and ferocity during Nigeria's military dictatorship, which helped bring about democracy in the country. But not all media are in this category; the majority of Nigeria's watchdog achievements can be attributed to the print media. For example, the former House of Representatives speaker resigned in 1999 when his age-related lies were discovered by the media (Apata & Ogunwuyi, 2019). Olusegun Obasanjo's plan to convince the National Assembly to amend the constitution to give him a third term in office was made public by the print media. The public has been made aware of multiple cases of financial theft, government corruption, and misconduct by public servants, many of which were reported in the print media.

When Ojomo (2009, p. 11) said, "This is the primary function of the electronic media in any society, yet it is the area where the Nigerian broadcast media have failed the most", he may have been inspired by the conspicuous lack of watchdog reporting in the broadcast media. The Federal Republic of Nigeria's Constitution declares in Section 22 that "the press, radio, television, and other agencies of the mass media shall at all times be free to uphold the responsibility and accountability of the government to the people and uphold the fundamental objectives contained in this chapter" (Aondover et al., 2021). By acting as a watchdog for society, this clause has explicitly equipped all media to fulfil its role as the Fourth Estate. This demonstrates the significance of this role even more.

The broadcast media's failure to carry out its role as a watchdog has been attributed to "the long monopoly of government ownership of the broadcast media" over time (Ojomo, 2009, p. 11). Others attributed it to a variety of laws and broadcast regulations that limit the freedom of the media, in addition to the absence of a law providing unrestricted access to information that is important to the general public. The Nigerian public expected greater results when the government deregulated broadcast media in 1992, even though those arguments have been shown to be valid.

On May 28, 2011, former president Goodluck Jonathan signed the Freedom of Information Act, which had been in the national assembly for many years. It was anticipated that the passing of this law would enhance journalists' greater access to information (Oberiri, 2016). The law provided for the public to have more access to information that would not have otherwise been available. The evidence thus far has been variable. Nonetheless, broadcast media continues to underperform as a watchdog. This might have affected people's use of social media to bridge the perceived gap.

The Media as Watchdog

The media's watchdog role as the fourth estate of the realm stems from the understanding of their primary duty to spread important information and influence the acceptance, formation, and expression of public opinion. The concept of the media as a watchdog, according to Onyemaobi (2018), gives an organisation the responsibility of monitoring, looking into, defending, exposing, and putting an end to wrongdoings while furthering the rights and interests of the general public. As part of this responsibility, the media educates the public about political, social, economic, and environmental issues. They set agendas and mould public views by providing the public with the thorough and essential information they need to make informed judgments.

As Oso (2013) notes, a free media outlet is one that serves as a watchdog. He stated that they couldn't allow any demands that would hinder their advancement or allow any interference, either from the outside or the inside. This knowledge might have impacted Oso's (2013) assertion that, even in developing democracies like Nigeria, the significance of this role motivated constitutional provisions, allowing the media to hold the government accountable to the people. The watchdog position is widely acknowledged by both journalists and audience members as the most vital and significant duty played by the media in a democratic society. Shardow and Asare (2016) concurred with Oso's evaluation when they said that a free media is necessary to guarantee that authorities successfully carry out their duties to the people.

It is evident that the media's capacity to act as a watchdog has declined in many regions of the world (Munoyiwarwa, 2018). The continued and successful execution of the role requires a dedicated, competent, and passionate breed of journalists who are willing to put the public interest ahead of all else. Nonetheless, there exist alternative explanations for the absence of watchdog journalism in the media. For instance, Oso (2013) assessed how effective the media is as a watchdog and concluded that financial and political benefits have lessened its efficacy, as seen by the commercialisation of media services. He believes that these interests have come to define and control the media's operational activities. As a result, as Oso stated, these interests have successfully taken over the media, undermining its ability and resolve to serve as strong watchdogs. They may still bark once in a while, but they are far less likely to bite now. Waisbord (2015) presented compelling evidence regarding the impact of economic matters. He made the case that news organisations established for profit are usually just unwilling to devote their often-limited resources to covering stories that do so; instead, they would rather stick to routine reporting, which mostly consists of repeating what the authorities say without going into great detail.

Coronel (2010) stated that independent media are more impacted by economic factors than government-owned ones. Private media companies will logically have more freedom to carry out their watchdog responsibilities, but they are frequently more likely to be market slaves than government media, which are obligated to carry out the government's propaganda since they are solely owned by the government (Endong, 2017). In nations like Malaysia, the government's control of the media and the resulting restrictions on freedom have made it less effective as a watchdog.

Access to information that is protected by some sort of legal framework could be important. The majority of Western democracies are supported by rules that encourage the pursuit of knowledge, even information that those in positions of power would prefer to keep secret. One of the key factors influencing media freedom is the ability to demand and obtain information. Access to information, according to Waisbord (2015), is a crucial component of watchdog journalism. He emphasised that only having content available is insufficient for watchdog journalism, saying that having legal assistance and strategies that make information easier to acquire is essential. The lack of freedom of information rules in many countries, especially developing countries, has hampered the media.

The media has been held up as the symbol or emblem for demanding accountability in many areas of the world, and in many places where it has become an integral element of journalism, it has helped to strengthen democracy by promoting and cultivating an attitude of openness and responsibility. Therefore, a continuous reduction in or absence of watchdog journalism has a significant negative influence on democracy in addition to the media's credibility and reliability (Kunia & Othman, 2019).

Nigerian Media and the Watchdog Function

Media under colonial and military rule in Nigeria were instrumental in the nation's democratic and independent transition. Strict laws like Decree No. 4 of 1984, for example, made media reports that exposed military regimes or their officials to public scrutiny and criticism illegal. Despite these restrictions, journalists like Dele Giwa and Ray Ekpu made it their mission to use their platforms to call for good governance by criticising and detailing some of the military administration's policies, plans, and actions that were counterproductive to freedom and the advancement of the country (Apata & Ogunwuyi, 2019). Their zeal and writing style enabled them to reveal multiple dishonest acts by the military government. In this regard, publications like *Newswatch, Tell,* The News and Tempo magazines showcased investigative journalism, which led to either prescription, confiscation of copies, arrest of their journalists and closures. Newspapers like *The Punch* and *The Guardian,* and television stations like Channels Television, and Arise Television and AIT are among those sanctioned by regulatory agencies or directly by the government under military rule.

Ojo (2007) asserted that when General Ibrahim Babangida was ruling as a military dictator, the print media, which included the Guardian, Concord, Punch, and Tell magazine, resorted to surreptitiously questioning public officials, searching for sensitive materials, and finding a way to obtain official records. But the administration took countermeasures. Some editors were detained, while others were even banned. To reveal the totalitarian objective of the administrations, the journalists persisted and continued to employ a variety of underground sources. The majority of these decisions were extremely dangerous, yet such journalism helped in 1999's transition to democracy.

The government tried to control the media during most of the military era. However, in 1992, and well before the return to democratic governance in 1999, the media was deregulated to enable private ownership, albeit with stringent regulations (Aginam, 2010). The government had such a tight grip on broadcast media because of its reach and capacity for direct and real-time communication with various audiences. The preferred and most often used method of reaching more people was, therefore, the broadcast media, due to its general affordability and other benefits. The government's monopoly of electronic media was because of its usefulness in the dissemination of propaganda to a wider segment of the populace. The government's arguably less stringent attitude toward watchdog journalism can be attributed to the very long monopoly it held on broadcast media.

The ensuing democratic system witnessed lesser evidence of hegemony and more plurality through the rise in private print and broadcast media ownership, which in turn led to increased diversity in media representations. A return to mainstream attention of formerly restrained media and journalists characterised the early years. Many returned, more energised and prepared to carry out their democratic responsibilities to the populace. Newspapers reorganised, restructured, and gained visibility in defining the tone and expectations and setting agendas as the new democratic dispensation unfolded.

By establishing agendas, critiquing, and promoting good governance, the media was able to checkmate the government throughout this period. Print media published a number of scoops. The media exposed Salisu Abubakar, the first Democratic speaker of the House of Representatives, for, among other things, lying about his age. Because of this, he resigned. President Obasanjo's plan to gain a third term in office was unearthed and exposed by the media (Apata & Ogunwuyi, 2019) in 2017, when a minister was forced to resign when issues arose over her credentials. Premium Times, an online newspaper, investigated this. In addition to providing extensive coverage and agenda-setting, the media has done remarkable reporting on corruption, misappropriation, and violations of human rights.

The Nigerian media, by protecting public interest through giving the public access to sufficient in-depth and pertinent information, have enabled them to make educated judgments that would ensure the people's wishes are carried out by the officials they elected. Amodu et al. (2016) agreed that it is the media's job and responsibility to, among others, inform the public about governance by covering government operations. The media has done a respectable job of informing the people in that area. However, the Nigerian media, like many other media outlets throughout the world, is becoming profit-oriented, with its "watchdog" role being subordinated to the quest for financial sustainability.

Media ownership structure and watchdog function may both play a significant impact in media independence. According to Ali (2015), the deregulation of broadcast media in Africa has not actually improved media freedom through media pluralism but rather worked to further the political agendas of the wealthy and powerful. According to Ali, there are restrictions on the media in certain countries, but they nevertheless have very independent media. He reached this conclusion by contrasting press freedom and media ownership in Africa with those in the U.S. and the UK.

Deregulation has made the Nigerian media more diverse and independent, raising the question of how truly independent it is. According to Oberiri (2017), stringent and oppressive media regulations are more important for determining press freedom than media ownership. He argued that while being in a democracy, rules and decrees that have been used to censor and persecute the media since the military era continue to subtly surface in the ways and means by which journalists practice self-censorship. He asserts that although press freedom is guaranteed by the Nigerian constitution, there are no official safeguards. According to Oberiri, the 1999 constitution's provision is counterproductive. The 1999 Constitution's Section 39 qualifies and purposefully limits press freedom. Subsection two of section 39 imposes prior restrictions on the ownership of the media used for the exercise of freedom of speech, especially with regard to broadcast media. He contends that judicial pressure continually tramples on Nigeria's media independence as a result.

Similarly, Chukwu (2018, p. 32) asserted that "there is no explicit or clear constitutional framework for freedom of information and good journalism practice in Nigeria. Instead, a great number of laws are developed to obstruct the latter". He also lamented that section 22, which guarantees free speech and outlines the obligations of the media, did not offer the necessary legal protections for the journalistic industry. As Chukwu noted, a better and corruption-free society will result from clearly enshrining press freedom in the constitution and evaluating and eliminating "any existing legislation which tries to excessively strangulate this right".

According to Apata and Ogunwuyi (2019), the media is undervaluing its function and performing comparatively poorly at a time when it is required to meet the public demand to fulfil its watchdog responsibilities. The media today reflects the corruption that has engulfed the Nigerian government. The media, according to him, is "a hotbed of corrupt and sharp practices". Endong (2017) claims that due to financial considerations and a lack of commitment to professional ethics, the media, particularly those under government control, have evolved into straightforward instruments for advancing governmental objectives without being scrutinised or questioned. Politicians and other powerful individuals can, in reality, invest in the media due to economic considerations, including the lack of funding for investigative stories and the inadequate capital bases at media companies. Due to their investments, they have a stake in the media, which prevents the media from publishing or reporting anything negative about them.

Chapter Four
Investigative Journalism

The term "investigative journalism" has several definitions. It is also known as public interest journalism, muckraking journalism, advocacy journalism, expose journalism, adversarial journalism, watchdog journalism, in-depth journalism, and journalism of outrage. The various definitions of these names reveal a range of ideas. For the broader public, investigative journalism evokes images of reporting on crimes. Since research is necessary before the news can be written, some people consider all reporting to be investigative. But there are differences between investigative and daily journalism, especially when it comes to themes covered, depth, focus, and even information-gathering techniques.

There are persons in every community who are primarily interested in finding ways to circumvent the law in order to obtain contracts, financial gain, and other things. In such a system, shady acts might never come to the public's attention unless there is a diligent whistle-blower interested in creating an ideal system. Investigative reporting aims to expose this kind of unethical behaviour. Investigative reporting refers to media stories that reveal vices, irregularities, shady dealings, mismanagement of public finances, absenteeism, and all other kinds of behaviours that go against the foundational principles of a just government or society. It can occasionally be attributed to inefficiency in the government, political parties, businesses, organisations, clubs, charities, trade associations, and even the media (Munoriyarwa, 2018). The media may report on the majority of inquiries as scandals. For example, US President Richard Nixon was implicated in the Watergate scandal; Bill Clinton and Monica Lewinsky had extramarital affairs while he was in the White House; Dimeji Bankole was charged with purchasing a car for 550 million dollars; and Tafa Balogun was reported to have embezzled 17 billion dollars from the police pension fund. Salisu Buhari, the first Speaker of the Third Republic, was impeached for fabricating a degree from Toronto University (Ekhareafo et al., 2016).

Investigative journalism involves reporters delving thoroughly into a particular issue to look for wrongdoing, scrutinise corporate policies or legal requirements, or draw attention to emerging social, political, economic, or cultural trends. An investigative journalist or team of journalists may need to dedicate months or even years of research to a single problem. Unlike traditional reporting, which depends on materials from the government, non-governmental organisations, and other sources, investigative reporting is based on information that the reporter independently gathers. The approach tries to make public information that might otherwise be hidden, either intentionally or unintentionally (Houston, 2010).

The Concept of Investigative Journalism

Investigative reporting should first unearth fresh information about a single subject or concern. An inquiry ought to be unique and provide the audience with something new. It should provide "clear, direct, and indisputable proof with no hint of ambiguity," going beyond simple fact-checking.

The public interest, which is frequently distinguished from "national interest," should be its second goal. Governments occasionally invoke the public interest to defend illegal, risky, or unethical actions or to deter journalists from covering a serious issue (Kaplan, 2020). In journalism, serving the public interest implies learning about topics that are significant to a large portion of the population in order to safeguard their lives, health, property, and rights, ensure justice, and uphold the rule of law. The public should be able to trust this information and use it as a basis for decisions thus it must be objective.

Third, an investigation's findings should be the result of thorough, methodical study and comprehensive documentation that adheres to professional and ethical standards (Kaplan, 2020).

Fourth, finding the information and conducting the inquiry should be the responsibility of journalists or their teams. Investigative journalists are fact-checkers, analysts, and researchers. They organise and conduct the inquiry (Unaegbu, 2017). They ought to be at the forefront of the writing, editing, and difficult editorial judgment processes. Investigative journalism can be seen as the systematic, in-depth investigation and meticulous documentation of brand-new issues and problems by the journalist themselves or by their team, with the goal of serving the public interest by exposing institutional or systemic shortcomings in a variety of spheres of life.

Journalists who conduct investigations don't cover accusations. The phrase "it is alleged that Mr. Marshal stole one hundred dollars" is not used. They go away and conduct their investigation for a few weeks or months before returning with the information, records, and proof they require to be able to conclusively prove that Mr Marshal stole the money, how he did it, and why (Derek, 2005). There shouldn't be any room for error or misinterpretation in investigative journalism. If there is still uncertainty regarding the information that they have gathered, the journalist has not dug far enough. This means it is not yet time to publish the investigation.

While locating the facts is part of a journalist's job description, an investigation is not made by facts alone (Burgh, 2008). It's important to systematically connect scenes, people, events, and places. In order for facts to have significance, they must be placed in the appropriate context, allowing the general public to judge them based on their merits and ultimately make a difference.

Thus, investigative journalism necessitates that the reporter does a thorough investigation into an issue or topic of broad interest. A quality that is in the "public interest" is one that will either help a community (materially or through informed decision-making) if it is known or harm it if it is not. Sometimes, information that benefits one community might have negative effects on another. For example, forest inhabitants may demand higher prices if they are aware of the market value of the trees that logging companies are attempting to sell. Naturally, the logging industry is against this information becoming public since it would drive up the cost of trees. The narrative does not have to have a national influence; in fact, it is common to distinguish between "public interest" and "national interest". Governments occasionally employ the latter phrase to excuse risky, unlawful, or unethical behaviour or to dissuade journalists from covering a serious issue.

Completing an investigative report requires time. It must follow accepted guidelines for evidence and accuracy and go through specified phases of planning, investigation, and reporting. A journalist and, when available, his or her team's proactive efforts constitute the foundation of investigative reports. As a reaction to story tips, journalists formulate theories, organise additional research, choose the relevant questions, and then go out to investigate them (Kaplan, 2020). To go beyond merely confirming the tip, they need to collect evidence through in-person observation and analysis of the answers. The final story should either reassemble already existing material or integrate new information to communicate the significance of the information. One source can provide access to knowledge, insights, and fascinating discoveries that might otherwise remain undiscovered. But unless the data from that source is contrasted with data from other sources (including personal, documentary, and human), and its relevance is evaluated, it cannot be regarded as an investigation.

Functions of Investigative Journalism

Investigative reporting is a duty that the media has to society (Ekhareafo, et al., 2016). Such reports provide the following functions:

1. Aids in sanitising society and fostering moral consciousness;

2. Makes public institutions and the government more accountable;

3. Ridicules society's vices;

4. Aiding citizens in forming or settling on educated opinions about societal affairs and social institutions;

5. It aids in establishing social fairness and upholding order in government institutions;

6. Raises the credibility of the media;

7. Fulfils the watchdog purpose of the media;

8. In this capacity, it serves as society's conscience;

9. Draws readers and increases revenue;

10. Encourage social change;

11. It improves public life by bringing awareness and order; and

12. Encourages professionalism in media practices around the world.

Traits of an Investigative Reporter

Ogbeni in Ekhareafo et al., (2016, pp. 47-50) highlighted some of the following traits of an investigative journalist thus:

1. The capacity to perform well under pressure, internal or external.

2. The capacity to work long hours in demanding circumstances.

3. A nose for news: A reporter relies on breaking news thus he needs to be able to spot an incident that merits coverage. He should be able to find news from anyone, regardless of how significant or unimportant they may be.

4. Aggression with caution: This is an emotional outburst directed at people who disobey the law or otherwise disrupt the system.

5. Extraordinary patience or perseverance in your efforts: As a reporter, you must be persistent and willing to go above and beyond when looking for a story. Keep in mind that there are many different types of people, and while some may have news to share, others may not be eager to do it.

6. High integrity: Anyone going to equity must do so with clean hands. Since he is a by-product of such actions, a reporter cannot investigate shady deals if he lacks moral character or integrity. As a result, the reporter must always display uprightness.

7. Accuracy: It is the reporter's aptitude to, among others, state facts, figures, names, times, numbers. Accurately and without embellishment or distortion.

8. Ethical sense of judgment: Every profession has rules governing the conduct of its members in terms of obligation and ethical behaviour. All people who do journalism are subject to strict requirements because journalism includes a kind of trust. You should adhere to the principles of journalism's code of ethics and stay informed about them. This is so that people understand that journalism is more than just writing news.

9. Knowledge of working tools: In order to make your job easier, you not only need to have some tools, but you also need to know how to utilise them. A computer and camera are some of these. In reality, it would be strange for a reporter in this day of computer-assisted journalism to lack computer literacy and knowledge of how to conduct an internet search. Additionally, knowing how to use shorthand will be helpful.

10. Contact-making skills: As a reporter, it's important to be able to maintain contacts in addition to making new ones. Do not hate anyone since they might be your best source within a company — the office assistant or even the cleaner. Therefore, treat them with the same respect that you would their employer.

11. Courage: It has been asserted that courage is not the absence of fear but the victory over it. The reporter should have the capacity to deal with potentially perilous situations.

12. Exercising patience, logic, and care.

13. Versatility: A reporter needs to be knowledgeable about the beat they are given to cover. Consequently, you must be familiar with the area in which you are doing business. Spend additional time developing this quality because no journalism school will ever teach that. A competent reporter should also maintain a positive outlook, be optimistic, and be adaptive.

14. Effective written and spoken communication in his medium: You must be fluent in the new language in order to perform your duties effectively. This will provide you with the opportunity to study as much as you can. Reporters are required to learn as much as they can about the subject they are given, such as politics, science, labour, economics, and history, given the current tendency toward specialization in news reporting.

15. Having a passion for public service: People can only improve society by working for it. The report's focus is to place issues in the public domain, exposing problems that are ruining society, and offering solutions to make things better.

16. A sense of humour: Journalism involves more than just bringing up serious subjects. It entails encouraging participants to unwind and laugh about their problems. Thus, a journalist's sense of humour will contribute to providing the amusement the public wants.

17. Trustworthiness: You must appreciate the trust that your sources have placed in you as an investigative journalist. No matter what, you must be able to safeguard your source. You should under no circumstances identify the information's source. If going to jail will help you defend the source, be ready to do it. For example, Nduka Irabor, Tunde Thompson, and Chris Anyanwu were among the journalists in Nigeria who received prison sentences for refusing to divulge the sources of information about military personnel who were shortlisted for ambassadorial positions.

18. Speed and accuracy: You must keep in mind that your media competes with others in the market as a reporter. You have to acquire and convey news quickly in order to meet a deadline. Keep in mind the adage "journalism is history in a rush". A crucial talent and attribute you'll need to succeed in the field is the ability to quickly gather and analyse news.

Table 1: The Difference between Conventional and Investigative Journalism

The table below shows the difference between conventional and investigative journalism.

Conventional Journalism	Investigative Journalism
Information gathered and reported on a fixed schedule (daily, weekly, monthly).	Information cannot be published until its consistency and completeness is assured.
Research completed quickly. No further research is done once story is completed.	Research continues until story is confirmed and may continue after its publication.
Story is based on the necessary minimal information. Can be very short.	Story based on the maximum amount of information, and can be very long.
Declaration of sources can substitute for documentation.	The reporting requires documentation to support or deny declaration of sources.
The good faith of sources is presumed, often without verification.	The good faith of sources cannot be presumed; no information may be used without verification.
Official sources offer information to the reporter freely.	Official information is often hidden from reporter, because its revelation may compromise interests, individuals, or institutions.

Reporters must accept official version of a story, though they may contrast it with other source materials.	Reporters may explicitly challenge or deny official version of a story, based on information from independent sources.
Sources are nearly always identified.	Sources often cannot be identified for the sake of their security
Reporting is seen as a reflection of the world, and the reporter does not hope for results beyond informing the public.	Reporting is aimed at penetrating or exposing a given situation to reform, denounce, or promote an example of a better way.
Reporting does not require a personal engagement from reporter.	Without a personal engagement from the reporter, the story will never be completed.
Reporter seeks to be objective, without bias, or judgement towards anyone in the story.	Reporter seeks to be fair and scrupulous towards the facts of the story, and on that basis designate its victims/survivors, "heroes", and wrongdoers.
Dramatic structure of the story is not primary as the story does not necessarily have an end because the news is continuous.	Dramatic structure is essential to its impact, and leads to a conclusion offered by reporter or source.
Errors in reporting are inevitable and are usually without grave consequences.	Errors expose the reporter to formal and informal sanctions, and can destroy the credibility of the reporter and the media.

Source: (IPC, 2023).

Challenges to Investigative Journalism

In a survey of US investigative journalists, Lanosga and Houston (2017) underlined the decline of investigative journalism as a global issue. The issues affecting this dwindling journalistic genre are categorised using a number of categories based on various examples, such as the threat of legal action, financial difficulties and budgetary constraints, violence against journalists, restrictive legislative frameworks, fake news, and misinformation. These elements, according to Kaplan (2008) have made the situation for investigative journalism insecure.

1. The Threat of Litigation

Investigative reporting has the ability to discredit and humiliate individuals being looked into, as well as to lead to legal action. There is always a possibility of being subjected to legal proceedings. For the majority of African media outlets and their journalists, life is a nightmare as a result of government officials' adoption of litigation due to investigative journalism's aggressive manner. Rosenthal (2012) contends that expensive legal action will always be a threat to investigative journalism. Many investigative media outlets cannot overlook the enormous risk that legal exposure poses to their financial stability. Ismail et al. (2017) claim that journalists refrain from publishing due to self-censorship and fear of legal action.

Lublinski et al (2016) assert that African newsrooms are more severely affected by the economic circumstances that present a challenge for media organisations since it has a detrimental effect on professionalism. Investigative journalists earn high compensation. However, some media organisations are unable to compensate them. With limited resources, it is challenging to maintain operations for investigative work. Investigations take time, and media outlets lack the funds to employ reporters who are unable to deliver stories every day. According to Oyedele et al (2018, p. 440), "Naturally, there are barriers working against investigative reporting in Nigeria, including low journalist compensation, limited capacity building by media companies, and other social and political-related factors".

Since advertising follows the audience, Kaplan (2008) claims that the shift to the internet has made investigative journalism more difficult. Noll (2000) noted that South African media has seen negative consequences from new digital technologies in terms of accessing and producing news as viewers shift to online places where news are available for free. In addition, the decrease in advertising has significantly limited investigative reporting in countries with totalitarian political systems.

Because of the disruption caused by less advertising, some media outlets now rely on donations to sustain their investigative reporting. Such donations help overcome limits imposed by restricted resources. According to Houston (2010), investigative journalists look to non-profit organisations for financial support. Scholars like Karppinen and Moe (2016) are concerned that the dependence on income and its consequent impact on media platforms in need jeopardise independence from outside pressures, a fundamental ethical principle for journalism. Investigative journalism is now a sponsored activity rather than what Kaplan (2020) refers to as "a neutral objective mirror of facts", due to investments.

Depending too heavily on donations creates ethical concerns about the funders' intentions and the objectivity of the media. There is risk of ethical behaviour being compromised by financial dependence on entities that employ investments to impose control. Donor-funded media training in Nigeria is skewed towards promoting the ideologies of foreign organisations, where investigative journalism would be nearly impossible without Western donor funding. According to Yusha'u (2009), funders who seek to further the goals of their organisations legitimise the worries about outside influence and the concern of whether investigative journalism exists theoretically.

2. Violence Aimed at Journalists

It is essential to recognise that journalism is also practised in societies where violence occurs. Violence can take many different forms, including harassment, bombing media houses, bodily assault, incarceration, and torture. According to Borins and Herst (2019), there has been persistent violence against journalists in the Global South, making investigative reporting there perilous. According to a 2007 study by Mudhai on barriers to investigative journalism in Nigeria, independent media outlets are more vulnerable when it comes to conducting investigative reporting. There are risks before, during, and after investigations. Saleh (2015) argues that the recurrent attacks and killings of journalists and other media professionals in Africa are justified by the fact that their jobs require them to uncover and report on the truth.

3. Restrictive Legislative Framework

Investigative journalism is hampered by governmental restrictions and legislation that are intended to penalise media professionals. Press freedom is severely restricted in most of the Global South because of laws that do not protect whistleblowers. Although the majority of restrictive legal frameworks are found in Africa, their application acts as a worldwide check on investigative reporting. According to Ismail et al. (2017), those obstructive laws are thought to be the cause of the suppression of investigative journalism. According to Al-Shami (2019), even the lack of legal safeguards for journalists against lawsuits is a barrier to the effective conduct of investigative journalism in the Arab world. For example, the regulations of Egypt neither allow for the protection of investigative journalists nor limit their activities.

Without whistleblowers, investigative journalism is a challenging endeavour. The use of national security laws by some countries to intimidate and suppress whistleblowers in an effort to restrict media freedom and keep the public ignorant, exists. While Nigerian journalists are enthusiastic about unearthing investigative stories, Yusha'u (2009) highlights the lack of legal protection and asserts that the absence of an independent judiciary deters them from looking into corruption.

4. The Era of Fake News and Misinformation

The spread of misinformation has rendered society vulnerable and can worsen the effects of catastrophic incidents. According to Wasserman (2020), the impact of false information on international politics has been so great that the media not only serves as a stage for political contests but has actively joined the fray. The effects of fake news raise concerns about what the media and journalists' future roles will be globally. Pseudo-investigative journalism is a complicit act in which journalists fail to seek to confirm the facts. Camaj (2016) discovered that media owners have been known to pressure journalists into engaging in false investigative journalism.

The fake news era, which is characterised by disinformation, and the popularity of pseudo-investigation, coexist. Hoax-based stories with edited content that spread rumours, hearsay, and incorrect facts are considered fake news. For financial gain or social influence, Klein and Wueller (2017, p. 5) note that "these false declarations of fact are frequently published on websites and spread through social media". It is clear that the motivations behind false news are both financial and ideological. According to Tandoc et al. (2018) ideologically driven fake news and misinformation are produced to discredit others who have opposing views. Governments, as well as people and organisations, have weaponised fake news. The lack of demand for facts, partisan ideology, and the debunking of opposing ideas are to blame for the prevalence of fake news.

The Future of Investigative Journalism

Investigative journalism will be conducted more and more online, according to Gearing (2014) and Harber (2020), and this should alter how practitioners approach their work. Investigative reporting has experienced a notable decline in traditional newsrooms and a rise in internet platforms. The internet has taken over the role of the media in setting agendas and censoring content. According to Fletcher and Park (2017), the internet has changed how people consume news, and nearly all conventional print and television news sources still have an online presence. According to Houston (2010), computer data mining will be the main subject of investigative journalism in the future, requiring collaboration with others, including IT specialists, software developers, and computer engineers.

In addition to the shift to online platforms, several strategies to improve investigative work have been proposed. Collaboration is one way to overcome the difficulties faced by investigative journalists, as seen in organisations like the Global Investigative Journalism Network and the Investigative Reporters and Editors. These partnerships are beneficial and could make investigative journalists stronger. In media systems that do not have the same degree of flexibility and independence as those in Western countries, the influence of relationships between organisations is far more significant. Initiatives to share investigative reports among media outlets as well as with international organisations have been launched in South Africa. A collaborative approach like this has advantages for content accessibility. However, there is no unanimity on the idea of working together. While global interconnectedness is welcomed, Wasserman (2018) worries that the fundamental issue of inequality and power dynamics in journalism may get less attention.

Consequently, the normative functions of investigative journalism are maintained in a world characterised by wrongdoing and a state that is less able to suppress corruption. This is guaranteed by the impact and the increased audience reach. To the extent that investigative journalists see fit, cooperation, content sharing, and internet usage must all be enhanced.

Steps to Investigative Journalism

It is important to note that the methods or suggestions offered here are not mutually exclusive; rather, they serve as a general framework for achieving the desired outcome. Even though there are established processes for investigating a story, they may not always be taken in chronological order. However, journalists should be aware that when conducting an investigation, they shouldn't start at the police station. Numerous cases that the police authorities have been covering up over time resulted in contentious situations without any hard proof to support them. For instance, the police have not identified who killed Chief Bola Ige, the Federal Government's then-attorney general.

It is crucial to note that every story has its own strategy; some may call for more than one reporter, and others might not. Some tales might take a while to develop into a reliable report, while others might be finished in a couple of days or weeks. This fundamental knowledge aids the reporter in choosing the optimal strategy for the story. It would aid him in acquiring the favourable disposition required for the story's successful conclusion. While some journalists lack determination and patience, others are willing to go above and beyond to complete a task. Ekhareafo et al., (2016, p. 53-58) outlined steps that could assist in the investigation irrespective of how long or short the investigation would take.

1. Preliminary Knowledge of the Subject or Issue through Research

When your editor asks you to conduct an investigation into what is happening in your neighbourhood, you must first conduct a preliminary analysis of the problem, the types of people you will interview, the locations and times of your informational visits, and the kinds of documents that may be necessary to obtain in-depth information. The purpose of the background knowledge is to organize or direct your goals and actions before you start the real research. With the intention of learning about the complexities involved in such an investigation, you can quickly search the internet for relevant cases. You can watch broadcast media and read newspapers on the case's signpost. The host community's response, the media-releases on press conferences, the statements made by a few principal officers, and the mention of other individuals or groups in the media can all be utilised to determine the case's supporting concerns.

It's important to note that the goal of the enquiry is to provide the reporter with background knowledge or information that will make the inquiry easier. Unplanned investigations are conducted in an unorganised fashion. Proper plans will give the reporter some insight into potential costs and investigational roadblocks. Therefore, it is essential to conduct a preliminary investigation to determine what the investigation's primary focus should be. The reporter would benefit from not wasting energy on unimportant things.

2. Starting the Investigation

The reporter can now head out into the field for the actual investigation after gathering the necessary information and background details about a case. In order to fully understand the atmosphere, tension, blame-shifting, and complexities of the case, the reporter must enter the scene of the events. The reporter must also interview the key players to determine what the issues are as part of this step. These visits allow the reporter to assess the harms, injustices, and destruction that led to the investigation in the first place. This is when the reporter conducts the in-depth interview that is necessary to cover the story. The information gleaned from the interview gives the hint that could likely inform the analysis of pertinent documents to see the relationship between the issues and the likely facts that may proceed where it is necessary for him to conduct a content analysis.

When conducting the interview, the reporter should pay attention to the interviewee's body language to understand how he or she is responding to the questions; such reactions could lead him to doubt the veracity of the assertion.

3. Confer with Relevant Authorities

Regulatory agencies oversee every aspect of national life. For example, the National Broadcasting Commission (NBC) oversees broadcasting and handles issues and conflicts in the broadcast media; the Nigerian Press Council (NPC) oversees print media; the Economic and Financial Crimes Commission (EFCC) handles financial fraud, public office theft, economic fraud, and other crimes; the Nigerian Police force handles any criminal matters that arise in society; the Central Bank of Nigeria (CBN) oversees financial regulation; the Nigeria Deposit Insurance Corporation (NDIC) oversees the nation's insurance industry.

A corresponding authority must be consulted for every crime or issue that warrants inquiry in order to determine the validity of the allegation and the extent of the regulator's involvement. In the event of egregious misconduct at a university, for example, the administration has the authority to convene a panel to investigate the matter or to call individuals before the disciplinary committee. It cannot stand unless the decision of the disciplinary committee is reversed by the school's governing council. Inquiries on financial fraud cases in any organisation should be sent to the Nigerian Police's fraud unit or the EFCC. The main goal is to present the story's official stance or account. In an investigation, the investigator's job is not to find someone guilty; rather, they should look for evidence that can help the public determine who or how a crime was committed.

In addition to regulatory agencies, there are other professional bodies whose legal expertise is necessary to crack open the case of an investigation. The key is to deconstruct complex subjects into clear and complete knowledge. In a report, they might aid in locating the lost bond. Through his understanding of bookkeeping, a competent accountant could prove the financial fraud in a financial statement.

It is instructive to mention here that investigators from the government may be involved. The police become an essential part of the case when a police officer is involved in extra-judicial killing. This will not deter the reporter from questioning the officers in any way. The point is that a journalist may still ask questions about a subject even if an authority has a conflict of interest in the answer.

4. Re-Examine Your Facts and Sources

When doing an investigation, it is not sufficient to conduct interviews and review documents; once a reporter double-checks the facts and re-examines his sources, he becomes critical of the facts and questions the missing pieces of information from what was said. Depending on the medium, the reporter must make sure that any legal obstacles, such as libel or defamation, are addressed. The facts could prompt the reporter to validate the veracity of a claim made by another source by consulting an impartial third party about what was said by others or to reaffirm what a source first claimed in light of the newly discovered information. In order to uphold justice, restore the reporter's and the media outlet's reputations, and prevent interviewees from claiming they were quoted erroneously, a re-examination of the facts is necessary.

5. Organise the Materials

Not all of the information collected and interviews held throughout an investigation will be useful for the inquiry's overall goal. While some may be clearly relevant, others might not contribute to the investigation's main goal. The reporter must choose and arrange the information in such a way as to result in a report that is significant. Here, the reporter carefully chooses the depositions, images, and injunctions obtained by the parties to the case. Writing the final report after organising the necessary resources is less difficult.

6. *The Final Report*

The public and media audiences learn about the controversy or expose it through this report. The final report provides a thorough explanation of what transpired, how it transpired, the conspiracies engaged in by various individuals involved in the case, and how the case unravelled. The reporter ensures proper links by doing this and organising the article in a comprehensible way. At this point, the journalist should include relevant photos to back up a claim. After a specific claim, an opposing viewpoint on the matter should be presented. Sources should always be cited, and any pertinent documents should be included as an addendum to the main point. The presentation of allegations and denials gives the report a balanced perspective. So that the public can form educated opinions based on the facts, statements of fact should be kept separate from statements of opinion. A well-written report will not only accomplish its goal but also boost the reporter's and the organisation's credibility.

Chapter Five
Political Journalism and Reporting

Politics depends on news to survive, so it needs the right kind of "blood" to grow and go in the right direction (Tunstall, 2024). In this case, considering the right kind of news is essentially in the interest of society as a whole in order to witness political development. Because of this, Brown and Udomisor (2015) observed that covering politics takes up a significant amount of the news media's time and resources. The ups and downs, personality conflicts, tussles, and party vicissitudes shape the political process and institutions that the media are compelled to cover, in addition to the pervasive policies and actions of the government. This has also led Kuhn and Nielsen (2014) to assert that political journalism is seen in its self-concept as a crucial component of democratic politics and at the very core of the journalistic vocation.

The historic notion of the "fourth estate", ascribed to the eighteenth-century conservative politician and philosopher Edmund Burke, continues to capture the essence of political journalism both as an ideal and, to some extent, as a reality. This exemplifies one of the primary roles of journalism in contemporary society: acting as the "watchdog" of the people over governmental actions (Gómez-García & Hera, 2023). The idea of the "watchdog" relates to the capacity of journalists to report on events as impartial observers with no stake in either side of a dispute, especially when the government is incompetent or corrupt. Kuhn and Nielsen (2014) corroborate that journalism is still at the core of politics in today's world, for better or worse.

Political journalism is a broad field of journalism that involves coverage of all aspects of politics and political science, even if the term is usually limited to reporting on civil governments and political power. The objective is to provide voters with the necessary information to form their own judgments and engage in local, state, or federal problems that affect them. In political journalism, it is the duty of journalists to enlighten the public on the activities and projects of politicians. Journalists need to ask the following questions of the people in charge and chosen to represent us:

i.   Are the politicians formulating economic policies which are workable?

ii. Do politicians tend to make decisions that are in the best interests of themselves, their allies, or the general public?

iii. Are the politicians making enough efforts to address the issues facing the nation?

iv.   Do they draft laws and rules that protect our safety and security?

v.   Are they creating policies that will raise people's standards of living?

vi.   Do they consider the long term, or are they purely focused on the here and now?

Political journalists face many challenges, yet they play a vital role in contemporary society. According to Kuhn and Neveu (2002), journalists are usually portrayed as being torn between the powerful influence of professionalised political sources on the one hand, and the necessity to draw audiences and the weight of popular opinion on the other. They also go on to show how journalists seem to be victims in this environment, destined to take action only in reaction to various situations that diminish their professional and intellectual liberty.

The gathering, assembling, and dissemination of news are tasks that fall within the responsibility of the journalist as a professional. They also set the agenda for public action as a direct outcome of their function as opinion leaders (McQuail, 2003). In fact, they inspire society to work toward a set of common objectives. In Nigeria, for example, even in the danger of their lives, the media was crucial in inspiring the populace to support the country's goal of constructing a democratic society.

Within the context of professional obligations, the journalist holds a crucial position in any media business. When it is known that the mass media provide the broadest and quickest means of conveying information, this role is more clearly understood (McQuail, 2002). They have an impact on social mediation, perception construction, and opinion formation. They influence social reality while serving as a mirror through which society might see itself. They give opposing organisations a free platform to voice their thoughts or solicit support, especially in a multi-party democracy like Nigeria. In this regard, it should be emphasised that the struggle for dominance is fierce and that the journalist frequently chooses the winning viewpoint.

Political News Reporting

Political news reporting is the independent analysis and presentation of political information by news media using media logic as opposed to political logic, as well as the adaptation of political actors to this media environment. As political news reporters, journalists are expected to be neutral judges who cover and report on politics without having any political preferences or biases (Onwubere, 2016). Political reporting is governed and scrutinised; it does not take place in a vacuum. A set of guidelines for political journalism was released by Ghana's National Media Commission in 2008. The recommendations urge the use of "peace-angle journalism" in political communication to encourage mature debate on the factors that lead to conflict and to highlight the chances for peacebuilding.

The following are some of the things that the reporter can attend to help get his/her feet wet as a political reporter:

i. Participating in government-organised public gatherings. He will learn a lot about government and how it functions from what he hears and sees at these meetings;

ii. Election-related rally meetings;

iii. Trials and court appearances or hearings; and

iv. Press briefings.

Elements of Good Political Reporting

Some of the elements of good political reporting, according to Sadiq (2017) include:

i. It presents the information in a way that encourages participation in a democracy and helps people react to the news;

ii. It provides background information and context;

iii. It demonstrates "Why the audience should care";

iv. It draws attention to how politics and political activities affect people;

v. It provides simple information and avoids using technical language in the process;

vi. It employs all the best reporting practices, including thoroughness, specificity, accuracy, and reliable sources;

vii. There are numerous storytelling styles used in it: hard-news fashion. Good quotations and sound bites, human instances, and anecdotes;

viii. It facilitates educated decision-making; and

ix. It sheds light on the political and democratic process.

Political News Reporting in Nigeria

Political news reporting and commentary in Nigeria have been seen to be wholly reliant on the ownership structure of the media and the connections of the owners to the political system. The media has never served as an unbiased institution because most newspapers frequently advocate for one political party against another or for one region against another (Onwubere, 2016). She also claims that political reportage in Nigeria frequently displays media partiality.

Brown and Udomisor (2015) concluded that political concerns (news) in Nigeria were primarily presented in favour of the government and were not strongly reported or given importance by way of appealing placement or location in the newspaper. They continued by citing additional academic works that demonstrated how the Nigerian broadcast media during the Second Republic focused more of their coverage on the rivalry between political candidates than on outlining the issues and the candidates' positions on them.

In essence, political news reporting in Nigeria has not been unbiased or fundamentally helpful to the general public in fostering political consciousness and a healthy political culture. Political reporting is perhaps quite unbalanced. However, it is important to recognise the Nigerian media for its important contribution to the political growth of the nation. The public's political awareness in Nigeria pre- and post-independence was aided by news and political concerns covered and examined by the media, particularly the newspaper. Without a doubt, the media's function contributes to the realisation of independence and, in turn, to the democratisation of the nation's polity.

Principles of Political Reporting

The most crucial thing to remember about politics is that it involves people—politicians who make decisions, government employees who execute their directives, and most importantly, the individuals impacted by those decisions. Serving these audiences is one of the ways a writer or journalist may bring balance and maintain objectivity. They equip them with the information necessary for participating in discussions and casting ballots for the candidates who will best represent their interests. Reporters shouldn't be writing for politicians or other public officials who are interested in certain subjects; they should already be aware of what is happening. A journalist should always consider how a political story will impact his or her readers' or listeners' lives before reporting it.

Politics reporting is also done for another cause. If someone informs the populace of what is occurring, they are free to respond. They have the option of writing letters to the editor or addressing politicians and other public officials directly to voice their thoughts and views. In this manner, persons in positions of authority are aware of the opinions of the populace. In any democracy, this is crucial.

According to Tilak and Vidyapeeth (2020), some of the principles of political reporting include the following:

1. *Clearly explain events and issues:* One of a journalist's key responsibilities is to clearly describe events and issues so that readers or listeners may understand and value them. They will present their readers or listeners with a shattered view of the world if they merely describe what occurs or what is stated. They must also be aware of the causes and effects of events. They must always contextualise events and problems in their narratives by illustrating how they affect the people.

2. *Explanation, not advice:* There is a significant distinction between outlining what happened and offering suggestions for how to change the circumstances. Clearly, one of the journalist's responsibilities is explanation. Leave the political activist or subject-matter authority to offer advice. As a journalist, you must report on many viewpoints without passing judgment on them in order to remain neutral.

3. *Be aware of your audience:* As with every aspect of the news, it's critical that reporters and journalists are aware of their viewers or readers. Once they have determined their audience's overall level of interest and comprehension, they can adjust their news-telling approach while always keeping in mind that they should strive to inform both the educated and less-informed parts of the audience.

4. The fact that some civilisations and communities are more "political" than others ought to be mentioned here. This indicates that they are more aware of politics at play in issues than members of some other communities. The problems that reporters should cover and how they should cover them will be determined with some assistance from the overall level of political knowledge in the area. It is not appropriate to force readers or listeners to care about politics. Even so, it shouldn't stop children from learning about political news that pertains to issues that have an impact on their daily lives.

5. *Be cautious:* It might sound obvious, but keep in mind that reporters can't believe everything they are told about politics. Always be on the lookout for lies, especially when someone is making promises or bragging about their accomplishments. Reporters should interpret a politician's or political activist's comments as personal advertisements when they are made only for image purposes (or to stay in the public spotlight for the next election). When they discuss a current event, you should check to see if their insights advance the public's comprehension of the situation. If so, that is breaking news. If not, it is simply a personal advertisement.

6. *Develop sources and contacts:* Even while journalists may have doubts about the motivations of politicians, they should still make efforts to network widely among them. They might need to set aside the fact that they don't agree with a politician's politics or ideology. They ought

to assess politicians equally, regardless of whether they like them or not. Every time someone speaks on a subject, a reporter must ask:

- Do they have the authority to put what they are saying into action? Can they actually put words into action?

- Do they have the ability to influence public opinion?

- Does their specific remark improve your audience's comprehension of the problem?

7. *Maintain source confidentiality:* Political journalists have a responsibility to uphold source confidentiality since they must deal with opposing viewpoints. Any promises they make to keep a specific piece of information to themselves must be kept. Unless they are certain that their adversary won't mind, they shouldn't divulge to the interviewer any information they have just obtained in private from them. People who feel comfortable speaking with them will frequently provide them with a wealth of information, both on and off the record.

8. *Understand the subject:* In all areas of journalism, subject knowledge and preparation are essential. Before conducting any interview, a journalist should be familiar with the topic, its history and most recent developments, the interviewee's political beliefs and background, and the political system that is relevant to the problem. Interviewing a local council leader on defence strategy, for instance, might be futile because defence is a federal or central government concern.

The reporters should always strive to formulate some probing inquiries. Some stories will require a more critical approach, while others could only require a clear explanation and a few follow-up questions to clarify certain elements. They must continuously keep asking questions until they receive a satisfactory response from the readers or listeners. The readers or listeners depend on them to know what kinds of questions they want answered because they are unable to ask the party leader, association chairman, or minister directly. They could believe that everyone already knows the solutions, but journalism does not aim to educate readers. As a journalist, they are there to inform the viewers or listeners. Thus, they will keep probing until they are confident that they will be pleased with the responses.

Therefore, reporters must maintain accurate records of any changes to political offices or governmental institutions. Make the appropriate updates to the newsroom reference file each time they produce an article about a political or governmental change. Get a complete list of the new ministers, for instance, if there is a cabinet reshuffle, and include it in the news desk file. Update the files frequently, and verify the contacts.

Chapter Six
Understanding Citizen Journalism

The era of the hypodermic needle has given way to a two-way, ubiquitous information and communication era with accompanying Information and Communication Technologies (ICTs), where everyone has access to the power of the media. Social media has contributed considerably to the growth of Nigeria's social scene. The state and a few media sources used to control the information monopoly, but the new equaliser is upending that. The proliferation of bloggers, critics, and commentators on social media is revealing untapped journalistic talent. These social activists are part of a new generation that has embraced cutting-edge technology and uses it for networking, sharing ideas, critising, and venting. Social media has allowed those without a voice to do so, and as a result, citizen power is expanding quickly.

You can now hear these voices if you register for an account on a social media platform such as Facebook or X (Twitter). Because of this, citizen journalism is an old activity with American origins. The public's general dissatisfaction with politics and civic affairs, coupled with the public's diminishing confidence in the news media, led to the emergence of a group of journalists who called themselves "citizen journalists", to cover the 1988 U.S. Presidential election. These journalists joined the public and civic journalism movement after realising their own limitations as journalists and the professional shortcomings of traditional media (Agboola, 2013).

Information and communication technologies, with their rapid advancement and pervasive application in society, have provided citizens with a means of actively engaging in their own countries' political processes. As a result of the widespread use of smartphones, computers, and the internet, it has become easier to quickly gather and disseminate information to any area in the world. The exponential advancement of technology is posing a threat to conventional forms of journalism today. User-generated media has supplanted conventional producer-to-consumer mass communication (Oladokun & Morah, 2013). This was made feasible by the accessibility of low-cost, easily operated technology tools as well as societal movements that support media content creation.

Since citizen journalism first appeared in America in the eighteenth century, it has expanded and achieved wide recognition throughout both developed and developing nations of the world. For example, citizen journalism is already being actively practiced by Nigerians. Since the year 2000, many Nigerians have created several blogs, websites, and twitter (as it was ten known) accounts. As

Hassan et al. (2024) observed that Odili.net, which was founded in 2002, is at the forefront of Nigeria's usage of online media and the creation of blogs. The Nigerian Village Square (NVS) was added in 2003. In 2004, Nairaland was established in Lagos by 22-year-old unemployed graduate Seun Osewa, who also gave the currency its name. Other online media sites include Sahara Reporters, Africa.net, Naija Community, and Naijapals.com.

Although citizen journalism is a positive development for society, its practice is frequently hampered by problems with credibility, trust, and objectivity. For example, Suleiman (2015) observed that despite China's strict media regulation, citizen journalism is only partially accepted there. However, people cannot trust the information they obtain online unless it has been thoroughly vetted and determined to be accurate.

Position of Scholars on Citizen Journalism

The definition of "citizen journalism" is dynamic and ever-evolving. According to Banda (2010), citizen journalism is a rapidly emerging area of the media in which regular people report news or share their thoughts on events occurring in their neighbourhood. He goes on to say that it is news that has been produced for and by the people. Citizen journalism is essentially a people-centred journalistic approach that considers the interests of regular people.

Oladokun and Morah (2013) state that terms like "public", "participatory", "democratic", "guerrilla", or "street journalism" are used to allude to "citizen journalism". It is the notion that news and information should be actively gathered, reported, analysed, and disseminated by the general population. Agboola (2013) stated that citizen journalism emerged as a result of the democratisation of multi-media technologies by the people and for the people. New media technologies have made it possible to actively participate in the creation and dissemination of information as well as to represent the interests of the general public.

Using similar journalistic practices but different motivations and alternative sources of legitimacy than the traditional media or mainstream journalism, Radschi (2011) expands on the concept of citizen journalism, arguing that it is an alternative and activist form of news gathering and reporting that operates outside the conventional media institutions, often in response to the shortcomings in the professional journalistic field. This accurately sums up the current state of media operations in Nigeria, where the majority of media outlets are controlled by the government and are regularly utilized to advance the agendas of powerful individuals. Along with the restrictions on access, time, and perhaps hidden agendas in the presentation of one side of a story by traditional media reporting, the risk of skewing news will be rather diminished by citizen journalism.

Because of these limitations, citizen journalism enables anyone to report on and disseminate news in order to offer their own interpretation of the events (Agboola, 2013). Using blogs, X, and YouTube, citizen journalists have reported on topics of interest to local, national, and international populations, such as police brutality and government corruption. The concept behind citizen journalism is that anyone, from any background, can use the resources of modern technology and the internet's global reach to produce, supplement, or fact-check media.

Atton (2009, p. 268) stated that "independent media help ordinary citizens to become politically empowered". On this basis, she asserts that individuals can better represent themselves and their communities in the media ecosystem when they produce their own media. The goal of citizen media is not to promote citizenship through the state but rather through media activities that foster political identity and citizenship in daily life. Therefore, citizens can use their own self-managed media to get politically involved on their own terms and thereby become active participants in the political process rather than relying on the mass media to define the bounds of involvement.

From the foregoing, it is evident that citizen journalism is an alternative kind of journalism that uses modern communication technology to allow regular people to become involved and participate in the gathering and sharing of information. As a result, contemporary communication technology has brought about a paradigm change in the communication continuum where the old channels of communication had power over determining and defining the agenda for public discussion. For example, people can set the agenda, steer the conversation, and ultimately draw attention to significant issues that affect them with the use of a mobile phone. By doing this, the traditional channels of communication lose their monopoly on deciding what to communicate to an audience and how to report it.

The Emergence of Citizen Journalism in the World

Technological advancements in the journalism profession have led to a paradigm shift in the field of news collection and reporting, elevating citizen journalism to a prominent position. The term "citizen journalism" originated in the immediate aftermath of the South Asian Tsunami in December 2004, when images and personal accounts were highly commended for their distinctive contribution to traditional news coverage. Experts in communication, such as Atton (2009), have connected the 2004 birth of Web 2.0 to the uptake of citizen journalism. Web 2.0 refers to the capabilities that let people collaborate on, share, and publish content on web pages with ease. Examples of web 2.0 sites include wikis, blogs, social networking sites, and websites that share videos. With Web 2.0, people are regularly becoming active audiences rather than the typical passive ones. This is why Baran (2004) pointed out that although we frequently consider those who use media as audience members, the internet has users rather than audience members.

The attention age of journalism has been ushered in by the internet. According to Nwabueze (2011), the ability of people to rapidly generate and consume knowledge, as well as share it with the social media community on the internet, defines the attention age. The main takeaway is that the typical person can now communicate information all over the world. This authority has previously only been granted to major media outlets and news agencies. We are all readers because of Gutenberg. We were all observers, thanks to radio and television. Xerox turned us all into authors. We are all journalists, broadcasters, columnists, commenters, and critics, thanks to the internet.

The increasing pressure that citizen journalism has placed on the mainstream media is changing their responsibilities dramatically in today's society. At the moment, there are a lot of Weblogs, or blogs, that are either managed by Nigerians or offer a forum for Nigerians to voice their thoughts and significantly contribute to contentious issues being discussed by a user community. Among them are 360nobs.com, Topic.net, Notjustok.com, Ogbongeblog.com, and Klinreports.com. Since web-based applications are frequently used to obtain information on the internet, they also generate and disseminate information, thus the term "Prosumers".

Prosumer is a term that combines the terms producer and consumer. *Prosumer* refers to the idea that audiences are now active, equal participants in the mass communication industry rather than only passive customers. Daniel in Apejoye (2024) stated that businesses no longer have complete control over their products, brands, and messaging. Currently, customers in Nigeria are in charge (citizens). These are the citizen journalists: social media users, forum posters, social network users, and microbloggers who cover events as they happen and influence audiences at home and abroad. In 2023, the Nigerian Communications Commission reported that there were 86 million internet users in Nigeria and 190 million connected telephone lines, of which 145 million had full-life subscriptions. Numerous audience-driven online citizen journalism platforms, discussion forums, and social networking sites have attracted millions of Nigerian users. There is currently a lot of enthusiasm about the alleged empowering potential of citizen journalism (Apejoye, 2024).

Positive and Negative Influence of Citizen Journalism in Nigeria

Unquestionably, citizen journalism has been instrumental in democratising the media and global society. The idea that all potential users and customers should have equal access to the media by reducing, if not completely eliminating, professional and commercial hegemony has, up until now, been a pipe dream. Thanks to the internet and social media platforms, almost anyone with computer skills may now communicate with a large audience via blogs, internet groups, social networking sites, and other related channels.

With the internet and social networking sites, residents may now openly express their thoughts, expose any corrupt practices, and question those in charge regarding matters that directly impact them. These roles were evident during the 2019 general elections in Nigeria, where citizen journalists were occupied with providing and amusing the public by reporting the election results piece by piece in the various polling stations as soon as they were made public. This led to a notable reduction in the frequency and occurrence of election rigging, which included ballot box theft, bribery of election officials by party representatives, and result manipulation. Asuni and Frarris in Apejoye (2024) state that INEC received about 4,000 Tweets and 25 million hits on its website during the presidential election alone and that over 70,000 people were able to get in touch with the commission directly to report problems and ask about concerns. Nigerian politicians started to realise the importance of social media and the internet during and after the 2015 general elections. The use of information and communication technologies in the electioneering process began with the elections.

Due to the significant media coverage that citizen journalists who were there at the scene of the occurrence gave it in 2008, the incident involving the brutal assault on Ms Uzoma Okere by navy officers in Lagos attracted considerable attention from the general public and even the government. They recorded the incident on tape while it was happening and posted it online right away. Again, a Facebook group called Occupy Nigeria was established and utilised to coordinate the demonstration and keep protesters fully informed when the Nigerian federal government eliminated fuel subsidies. These are glaring indications that citizen journalism has become an established practice in Nigeria and that people are continuing to take advantage of the opportunities it has provided (Godwin et al., 2019).

The negative influence of citizen journalism depends on the motivation of the person or people engaged. Citizen journalism has its drawbacks. When the negative effects of citizen journalism are discussed in Nigeria, the event involving the unpleasant photos of the accident scene when a truck driver crushed to death 19 robbery victims along the Lagos-Ore Highway on July 31,

2009, immediately comes to mind. Unfortunately, in March 2010, the internet was filled with obscene photos of the incident, which occurred a year earlier but was made to appear recent. This sparked public debate and interest. The heist that was purported to have taken place on February 25, 2010, as published online by citizen journalists, was disputed by statements from security authorities and some of the individuals involved in the case, according to the reports. Ogbonna Onovo, the Inspector General of Police at the time, allegedly informed to Nigerian Best Forum (2010) that the event was a replay of a heist that took place on July 31, 2009, between Ore, in Ondo State, and Shagamu, in Ogun State, Nigeria.

The salt-water bath for the Ebola virus was another instance of citizen journalism's negative effects in Nigeria. People were exchanging texts on the same topic via WhatsApp, BBM, Facebook, Twitter, emails, and other platforms across Nigeria. These were a few typical examples of what can be regarded as a significant negative impact of citizen journalism on Nigerians. Thus, unethical reporting is more common in blogs than in mainstream media. Since information posted online by citizen journalists does not undergo editing, it is possible for X-rated, indecent, and other inappropriate items to be uploaded, which could expose vulnerable segments of the population to them.

Citizen Journalism Implication for Mainstream Journalism

People are now covering events and promoting materials quickly and readily; thanks to the internet and other modern technology devices. In Nigeria, citizen journalism is becoming more prevalent to the point where it now regularly provides news and other important information in the mainstream media. Because citizen journalism is participatory and real-time, it has given rise to new opportunities and significantly improved mainstream journalism in a number of ways. For instance, because they are time and budget-constrained, many mainstream media now rely on citizen journalists to provide them with information about events taking place in their locality. Citizen journalism has demonstrated its effectiveness as a component of news reporting and as an advantage for journalists and editors.

Philips, as described in Bayelsa Official Social Media Group (2015), claims that social media in some parts of Nigeria creates a new form of civic involvement that mixes traditional and social media. He went on to claim that reporters increasingly watch social media sites like Facebook, YouTube, and Twitter and include the voices of everyday people in their news reporting. In order to meet information and communication needs across fields and disciplines, computer communication has been combined with the internet, mobile phone technology, satellite communications, and other forms of communication to create a new media technology stage with multimedia capabilities.

Citizen Journalism and Election Monitoring in Nigeria

Globally, citizen journalism has been used to monitor election outcomes in both developed and developing African countries, as well as to involve voters in political activity. The advent of social networking sites, brought about by the growth of the internet, is making it possible for public governance to become more transparent and democratic. Many organisations are beginning to recognise how these communication platforms might enhance public protests, political involvement, and even social mobilisation. In addition to the large number of Nigerians who have registered with social networking sites, discussion forums, and innumerable audience-driven online citizen journalism sites, many people in the country now own email accounts. News broadcasting is, therefore, not limited to the use of conventional communication methods. People across the country are now actively involved in producing and developing media content. Nigerians are no longer just passive media consumers as a result.

During the 2011 general elections, Nigeria tested the all-pervasive capabilities of new media technology. Prior to this, election activity monitoring was solely the responsibility of the traditional medium of communication. However, both traditional journalists and citizen journalists alike heavily utilised new media technology during the 2011 general election. Many Nigerians were using their Twitter accounts and Blackberries during the elections. They also mention Gbenga, a 33-year-old activist and IT consultant, who was part of the group that developed the Revoda smartphone application, which allowed voters to report materials that were delayed in arriving at their local polling stations and document intimidations.

In a related incident, voters were given BlackBerry pins via Twitter by the Independent National Electoral Commission (INEC) in order to use it for sending updates from the polls. Several Nigerians were able to report on the events in their various polling places during the elections via Facebook and Twitter. A woman who was shown by a citizen journalist on a YouTube video thumb-printing repeatedly on various ballot papers is one example that caught people's attention. She was affectionately referred to as "The last VoteBendor" on Twitter. This caught the attention of INEC (Apejoye, 2024).

Youths were mobilised by civil society organisations and groups to keep an eye on the election process at their individual polling places. For instance, during the elections, the Shehu Musa Yar'Adua Foundation set up a social media tracking centre where young people participated in monitoring election results across the entire nation. Civil society organisations have also established reporting channels through SMS, Twitter, websites, blogs, and phone lines. After receiving reports from the field during the election process, an Abuja-based civil society organisation established a civil society Election Situation Room. This room relayed information to INEC, the Police Service Commission, and the Nigerian police in turn.

Social media sites were formed by groups such as "Enough is Enough Nigeria", "Reclaim Naija", "Wongo", "I am Lagos", and numerous others to enable individuals to report occurrences relating to the election using text messages, voicemails, pictures, and videos. The Reclaim Naija campaign, which started in March 2011, demonstrated a change in mindset when hundreds of local market vendors, hair stylists, and battery chargers, among others,f rose to their feet, held up their cellphones, and declared, "The power is in our hands".

Nigerians watched the elections on their mobile phones. New media technologies have had a bigger influence on the elections. For example, for the first time in the country's history, the 2011 general elections in Nigeria were monitored by many Nigerians. This was courtesy of the 87 million smartphones that the country's citizens, the majority of whom were young and social media savvy (potential citizen journalists), had. This significant accomplishment contributed in part to the election's transparency (Agboola, 2013).

With the help of modern media tools at Nigerians' disposal, numerous electoral frauds and malpractices were revealed. One noteworthy occurrence, for instance, occurred in Imo State during the 2011 elections. During the early hours of April 9, a Nigerian citizen named Miss Chika tweeted that one of the senatorial candidates, Kema Chikwe, was orchestrating the completion of results sheets in a private residence. Trained observers were dispatched from two civil society organisation groups to confirm the tweet once they were notified. The day's events were tweeted incessantly by residents both domestically and internationally. By the conclusion of voting, Chika Anyanwu defeated Kema Chikwe, and word of the victory spread swiftly. Utilising social media to its fullest degree helps to reduce instances of election result tampering and made the process more transparent. Therefore, it is possible that the 2011 and 2015 elections would go down in history as a pivotal election that marked the entry of new media technology into Nigerian politics.

The Cause of the Rise of Citizen Journalism in Nigeria

Political circumstances played a significant role in the rise of citizen journalism in Nigeria. After the military relinquished control, the mainstream media swiftly stopped covering progressive and investigative stories and getting involved in the community. The period of time when journalists continued to write covertly and in defiance of proscription and anti-media laws is known as "guerilla journalism" (Dare, 2010). The demand for accountability, a return to democratic governance, and adherence to the rule of law and human rights was significantly facilitated by the media. Later, these factors evolved into the very ones that contemporary citizen journalism currently depends on. The media did not sustain this trend in 1999, when democracy was restored. The media and civic society, thinking their jobs were done, became less active.

The audience began to doubt the effectiveness of the media in the absence of fearless investigative reporting. An audience that was growing further distant from the traditional media was questioning its objectivity and neutrality. According to Williams in Agboola (2013, p. 227), "Journalism is too serious a business to be left to professional journalists", in the same way that fighting wars is too serious a business to be left to soldiers, and politics is too sacred a calling to be left to politicians. As history has demonstrated, any profession that discredits itself or abandons its sacred obligations invites outside intervention. Nature detests a vacuum.

The audience dispersed to investigate new websites for citizen journalism, especially the discussion forums where they could engage in varying degrees of discourse. According to Olaito (2010 p. 17), "Following five years of steadfastly advocating for a new world where the voices of the voiceless, the so-called underdogs who could not afford the cost of putting their opinions on the pages of the regular media, now have a new found love, opportunities in the social media platforms-premised on the need to communicate, share opinions in an environment that encourages cordiality and relationship building".

Criticisms and Critical Environment of Citizen Journalism in Nigeria

Some critics of citizen journalism have voiced their concerns. There are those who maintain that citizen journalism is not truthful. Some contend that political instability, ethnic and religious conflicts, and social unrest are fueled by citizen journalism. The height of this criticism was during the nationwide demonstrations that followed the withdrawal of fuel subsidies in January 2012. Some people thought that citizen journalists had given the activists false information, which led them to band together to oppose the government. Nevertheless, given that the fuel pump price significantly dropped, it was believed that the protest's goal had been partially met.

Citizen journalism has been criticised for trivialising important national issues, such as national catastrophe. The actions of citizen journalists came under scrutiny during the Dana Airline crash on June 3, 2012, especially from national politicians. It was said that while rescue workers were frantically searching for lives, citizen journalists were snapping and sharing graphic images on various social networks.

The capacity to be unbiased or free of prejudice is what constitutes objectivity. Journalism requires accurate, fair, and impartial reporting of issues and occurrences without adding or distorting information that could alter the investigation's conclusion or being influenced by the object of the investigation or the subject of the inquiry (reportage). It also has to do with distinguishing between fact and opinion (Uwakwe, 2005).

Therefore, there are other considerations that must be considered in order to achieve objectivity, including workplace dynamics and other exogenous elements that affect a person's internal psychological processes. The journalist's freedom to select the news and how to cover it without going against organisation policy is foremost among these rights. In spite of this, governments, media owners, and editors continue to conveniently order reporters around. Inferring that the "corporados" may exert a subtle influence over information by stressing some items more than others.

Media coverage of an issue or event is determined more by how profitable it is for the media owners than by the media's guiding principle of "let the public be informed". Media specialists like Ben Bagdikian, Magnus Enzensberger, and others have condemned the gatekeeping industry's invasive influence on the distribution of information and advocated for media democratisation and horizontal communication links at all societal levels. The political class and the media companies are both members of the oppressive group in society. Because of their dissatisfaction and discontentment with the institutional foundation of traditional media, the mass media's supporters now doubt the power of the media to influence politics. To ensure that their representations benefit others, participants must exercise critical thinking, pose insightful questions, and make an effort to understand the context. However, experts argue that the quality of any citizen journalism project depends on the opinions of those who choose to participate and that these programmes could act as safe havens for repetition and misinformation. Educause (2007) reports that citizen journalism has the potential to indirectly endorse:

> information that might be false, offensive, or lacking in credibility. As a result, a tool designed to increase the credibility of reporting may actually cause people to lose faith in the news. While ethical professional journalists take care to distinguish fact from opinion or speculation, many citizen journalists are less aware of the difference between a trustworthy report and unrestricted conjecture. Consumers of citizen journalism should be aware that, no matter how well-intentioned a citizen journalist may be, it is wise to read the news critically (p. 3).

It won't be out of place to claim that impartiality in the media, both traditional and citizen journalism, is nothing more than a remnant of antiquity and may never be achieved. Since the origins of Nigerian journalism, the country's media outlets have consistently produced speculative, subjective, or altered news that best suits the whims of those who spread it (Onyike et al., 2011). One of the reasons given for this was the media's lack of freedom and autonomy. The emergence of citizen journalism was hailed as the answer to the lack of objective journalism (reporting), but analysts contend that this media space has instead been plagued by scandalously packaged, speculative, and highly opinionated reports, many of which are replete with anecdotes that may be demeaning to certain segments of society.

Ethical Issues of Citizen Journalism Practice in Nigeria

The practice of journalism depends on ethics because they set acceptable parameters for professional conduct. It's critical to take into account the ethical issues brought up by the growth of online media. As with the printing press and printer made popular by Gutenberg, everyone is now effectively a journalist, thanks to the advent of the internet. Citizen journalism has made it possible for anyone to be a media creator, owner, and actor rather than just a passive information consumer (Ezeibe & Nwagwu, 2009). Citizen journalism is increasingly demeaning traditional forms of journalism. As a result, the public takes over professional journalism's function as an information provider. The following is a discussion of a few ethical issues:

1. *Plagiarism:* The practice of online journalism in Nigeria has significant difficulties due to the blatant lack of source attribution and, frequently, open plagiarism. The ethics of the journalism industry demand that all information sources be cited. In the event that the information is false or involves libel or defamation concerns, acknowledgement strengthens the credibility of the media and prevents it from becoming involved in legal disputes (Talabi, 2011). Online platforms today pull information from other sources and refuse to credit them.

2. *Accuracy:* Recently, concerns have been raised about the degree of authenticity of online stories, many of which have been proven to be false. Many websites are thought to be little more than rumour mills that publish unverified information. There is still scepticism about the calibre of journalism produced on the internet, despite efforts by online news outlets to break stories. That uncertainty might be used to describe the traditional media's ongoing refusal to acknowledge news sources other than the internet. Compared to those in the traditional media, the majority of the upcoming managers of online news media platforms lack basic journalistic training (Tijani, 2019).

Some of them are eager to break the news in an effort to boost traffic to their news sites and improve their market positioning and popularity, but they neglect to adhere to a strict editing process designed to guarantee accuracy.

3. *Obscenity:* Any statement or action that flagrantly violates morals is considered obscenity. Obscenity frequently appears in publications that feature nudity, sexual violence, or pornography (Greer & Mensing, 2016). This used to be frowned upon in the practice of journalism, but in recent years it has become increasingly common in online journalism, and regrettably, society no longer seems to find anything wrong with it. Online content that violates the public's sense of decency is frequently shared, as contrasted to content that adheres to ethical standards. This is really disturbing, particularly in light of the reporting on children and minors. Whether they are witnesses, defendants, or victims, children under the age of 16 who are connected to cases involving misdemeanours, cultism, sexual misconduct, and other related offences are not allowed to be named, identified, or interviewed by journalists under any circumstances. In an era of citizen journalism, profiles of children are uploaded online without taking into account the effects such actions would have on the lives and future of the children in question.

4. *Decency in Reportage:* This refers to maintaining ethical standards and showing respect for individuals and communities when reporting news stories. This concept is particularly crucial when covering sensitive issues such as humanitarian crises, conflicts, or personal tragedies.

Chapter Seven
Peace Journalism and Conflict Management

Conflict occurs occasionally in almost every society in the globe. Even at the individual level, disagreements about viewpoints and methods of approaching the issues generally lead to conflict. Conflict, therefore, exists in every human community and is inevitable (Owens-Ibie, 2016). Conflict by itself does not pose a threat to society, particularly when the parties engaged use it to promote their own civilisation. Conflict, however, only becomes harmful when it turns violent and destructive at the time it occurs. The majority of societies in the world are, in general, plagued by violent and destructive wars that have prevented them from moving forward and developing. This issue is particularly terrible in Africa, especially in light of the bloody hostilities that have ravaged the continent, from the Rwandan genocide to the conflicts in the Middle East.

Conflict typically entails struggle and competition over things that people and groups value. These things can either be made of material or not. The tangible things can include limited resources like money, work, political positions, and promotion in both private and public institutions. The intangible items could be things like culture, tradition, religion, and language. Disagreement, clash, collision, struggle, or contest between two or more parties are all considered forms of conflict. It can also be understood as a circumstance in which there are conflicting thoughts, feelings, opinions, or desires; a circumstance in which making a decision is challenging. However, depending on the goals of the parties involved, violent confrontations can sometimes take on an ethnic or religious colour, while other times, they can take on a political or regional colour.

In times of bloody war, religion has the power to be both a force for good and for evil. To gain support, defend their conduct, and claim "moral or religious superiority" over others, many parties to violent conflicts turn to religion or ethnic identities. One of the most frequent conflicts, especially in Nigeria, is ethno-religious conflict, which occurs frequently as people engage in violent conflict in the name of their faith. The current and ongoing religious, communal, and ethnic unrest and escalating interethnic animosity appear to indicate a decline in faith in the unity of the Nigerian nation and a turn toward ethnicity and particularism due to allegations of discrimination, marginalisation, and exploitation by some national community members (Malam, 2006).

In terms of belief, adherence, structure, expansion, and control of resources inside the Nigerian state, the two main religions in the country, Christianity and Islam, have, over the years, competed with one another. As a result, issues of fanaticism have echoed in the relationship between the two faiths, with reported cases of strife, chaos, and violence. According to Egwu (2013), ethnicity and religion are actual identities that people are willing to sacrifice their lives for. Religion for Nigerian people is a set of ideas and actions founded on faith, which are sacrosanct and defy rational analysis. As a result, it can very readily cause emotional reactions.

Despite being completely at odds with their core principles, these two religions have been at the centre of a religious crisis in Nigeria that has resulted in the destruction of both lives and property. They have been cited as culpable in diluting the very essence of Nigeria's nationhood rather than establishing peace, understanding, unity, and stability. Religious conflict, according to Egwu (2013), is the most terrible and hazardous experience, and any country that engages in it hardly lives. Both Christianity and Islam are critical components in the practice of Nigerian politics and are vigorously proselytised. The intense competition between Christians and Muslims is intense.

More than any other sort of division, religious dichotomization has been a significant problem in Nigeria. Religious unrest between Christians and Muslims occurred in Kaduna State, in 1985. In 1991, rioting in Bauchi State ruined the National Sports Festival that was taking place there at the time. Other examples include the ethnic and religious crisis in 1992 in Zangon-Kataf and the 1980–1982 Maitatsine riots in Kano. Interethnic fighting between the Fulani and the Karimjo in Taraba State in 1996, violence between the Hausa and Yoruba in Shagamu in 1999; conflict in the Okitipupa region of Ondo State from 1998 to 2000; Kano conflict in 1999–2000; Conflicts in the Taraba/Benue States, Wukari, Takum, in 1999–2002; inter-communal conflict between Aguleri and Umuleri in 2000 in Anambra state; conflict in Burutu local government in Delta State; and conflict in Modakeke in Osun state in 2000 and 2001; 2005, ethnic and religious tensions in Jos, Yelwa, Shandam; ethnic, religious, and political disputes in Jos, Plateau and Bauchi States between 2008 and 2011, Karimjo/Fulani interethnic conflict in the Ardo-kola region of Taraba State in 2011 (Yahaya, 2011). In a national broadcast, former military ruler Gen. Babangida referred to one of these religious riots as the "civilian equivalent of a coup".

Fundamentals of Peace Journalism

Since Johan Galtung first described peace journalism in the 1960s in his paper "The structure of foreign news", which questioned the prevailing journalistic style of the day, other academics have also examined the phenomena, with a large number of them concurring on certain essential elements. Broadly speaking, peace journalism is a journalistic approach that highlights stories in a way that encourages conflict analysis and a peaceful resolution.

Peace journalism, according to Lynch and McGoldrick (2005), is concerned with the choices editors and reporters make about what subjects to cover and how to present them in a way that inspires society at large to consider and value peaceful alternatives to violence. The evaluation standards established by Lynch and McGoldrick provide guidance on the types of attitudes and behaviours that peace journalists should try to avoid. These include the following: depicting a conflict as involving only two parties competing for a single goal; accepting sharp distinctions between "self" and "other"; treating a conflict as though it only exists in the location and during the time that violence is occurring; using evasive, emotive language to describe what has happened to individuals, demonising adjectives and labels, constantly focusing on what separates the parties, allowing parties (to a conflict) to define themselves by merely quoting their leaders' restatement of well-known demands or positions, and portraying an opinion or claim as fact.

Vukasovich (2012) has identified certain associated issues in relation to peace journalism. He claims that the goal of peace journalism is to reframe news, give voice to the voiceless, and create a common ground that unites rather than divides human civilisations in order to transform conflicts from their destructive paths into constructive ones.

Ten Commandments of Peace Journalism

Shinar (2007) has also outlined "Ten Commandments" for peace journalism, similar to Lynch and McGoldrick. These "commandments", he emphasised, are flexible and suggestive rather than exhaustive. They consist of:

1. Never reduce a human conflict to just two parties. Keep in mind that the grass suffers when two elephants fight. Take note of the pathetic grass.

2. Identify the views and interests of all parties to human conflicts. There is no single truth. There are many truths.

3. Avoid being held captive by a single information source, especially one that is controlled by a government.

4. Develop a healthy scepticism. Consider the fact that representation is reporting. People are biased by nature. The exceptions don't include you, your media outlet, or your sources.

5. To represent and strengthen the peacemakers and the underprivileged, give them a voice.

6.   When dealing with conflict, look for peaceful solutions rather than quick fixes.

7.   If your depiction of conflict issues fuels animosity and dualism, it may contribute to the issue.

8.   If you use the creative tensions in any human conflict to look for compromises and nonviolent solutions, your depiction of conflict problems can contribute to the solution.

9.   Always uphold the standards of objectivity, accuracy, and respect for human rights and dignity set forth by professional media ethics.

10. Set aside your own racial, national, or ideological prejudices in order to see and truthfully depict the parties to human disputes.

Some of Lynch and McGoldrick's recommendations can be observed in Vukasovich's 'commandments', and vice versa. For instance, both share the recommendation to avoid depicting a conflict as involving just two participants. This is crucial to note since the mainstream media frequently portrays conflicts as being between two powerful parties, such as the US/Coalition forces fighting Iraq or Israel fighting the Palestinians. Another similarity is the requirement to identify the opinions and objectives of all parties while acknowledging the multitude of realities that demand reporting. Additionally, avoid discussing or focusing on violence because that might contribute to the issue. They also concur that journalists should give everyone a voice rather than only reporting on entities that control information, such as governments.

The Emergence of Peace Journalism

The 1970s saw the emergence of peace journalism, for journalists to utilise as an example of how to avoid a value bias toward violence when reporting on war and conflict, Johan Galtung, a Norwegian sociologist, peace researcher, and activist, invented the notion of peace journalism. They went on to define peace journalism as the process by which editors and reporters decide which topics to cover and how to cover them, thereby presenting opportunities for society to think about and appreciate peaceful resolutions of disputes. It is a more comprehensive, equitable, and truthful way of telling tales because it integrates the ideas from the conflict, analysis, and transformation.

Lynch and McGoldrick (2005), who advocate for peace journalism, also said that war journalism focuses on apparent acts of violence and on the most obvious hardship a country faces. They observe that war journalism has a propensity to anticipate and report on violent tragedies in particular, it frequently employs traditional bureaucratic, formal expressions that emphasise the outsider's perspective. They contend that these represent a kind of authority-issued summons to action. Reversing all of these is peace journalism. According to Howard (2002), peace journalism does not confine its role to any specific stages of conflict but rather covers news during all stages, including the pre- and post-conflict phases.

As peace journalism assumes, the media can positively shift conflict away from violence by expanding the quantity and diversity of people whose views and viewpoints are shared, given credence, and respected. Peace journalists strive to consistently reject the simple view of violence, which often blames the cause to "the others" while emphasising that violence itself is the issue. By determining the parties, goals, and issues at hand from ethnic, historical, and cultural viewpoints, peace journalism addresses the formation of conflicts.

Lynch and McGoldrick (2005) explain that peace journalism's ultimate purpose is to improve for all sides the opportunity of exchanging perspectives as a method of discovering more effective strategies to change or end violent conflict. Since it investigates alternatives and fixes, peace journalism is concerned with contexts, backdrops, and the general, detrimental effects of violent conflicts. Peace journalism improves information flow and expands the spectrum of conflict resolution possibilities. Its focus is on a win-win approach that rejects basic dichotomies like good/evil or right/wrong.

Characteristics of Peace Journalism

Lynch and McGoldrick (2005) outline three characteristics of peace journalism as follows:

1. Bringing the idea of balance, fairness, and accuracy in reporting up to date through the use of conflict analysis and transformation;

2. Creating a new path and map that shows the relationships between journalists, their sources, the stories they cover, and the effects of their reporting - the ethics of journalistic involvement; and

3. Integrating a nonviolent and creative mindset into the practical work of daily reporting and editing.

Five Principles of Peace Journalism

Bassil (2014) stated that peace journalism is characterised by five main principles, which include:

a. Examining the backgrounds and conditions of conflict creation for all parties involved in the conflict, not just the two that are typically presented by the mainstream media;

b. Giving voice to the opinions of all rival groups at all levels;

c.   Coming up with innovative suggestions for growth, peace-making, peacekeeping, and conflict resolution. The media should support the parties in dispute to a peaceful conclusion in their reporting;

d.   Exposing lies, cover-up attempts, and culprits on all sides, as well as revealing and exposing abuses committed by and suffering inflicted upon individuals of all parties. Most of the time, if one is not killed after being discovered to have ties to this sect, one is lucky; and

e.   Paying attention to post-war growth and stories of peace. Because of this, becoming a successful journalist requires thorough training.

The Practice of Peace Journalism in Nigeria

Like other professions, journalism practice in Nigeria directly affects the populace and the entire nation. Media professionals are required to abide by the canons, often known as the journalistic code of ethics, which all practitioners must abide by and which members are expected to uphold without exception. However, Adaja (2012) noted that the practice of journalism in Nigeria has generated a lot of debate regarding whether to classify it as a trade or a profession. The profession is now open to everyone due to the unclear membership requirements (Aondover, 2017).

Thus, it has been challenging to control the level of journalism practice in Nigeria due to the lack of a mandatory qualifying exam. The actual professionalism of journalism practice in Nigeria is being hampered by these flaws. This has a significant impact for peace journalism, especially in the Northeast of Nigeria. Boko Haram's fury was directed at some media outlets and journalists because the sect thought that media coverage of conflicts was done in an unprofessional, one-sided manner (Owens-Ibie, 2016).

For example, in October 2011 shooters who were thought to be sect members killed Zakariyya Isa, a reporter for the Nigerian Television Authority in Maiduguri, was killed in a bombing at the farm centre police station in Kano in January 2012, Eneche Akogwu, a Kano State correspondent for Channels Television, was killed in a bombing at the same location in April 2012, and the sect also attacked the offices of *ThisDay* in Abuja and Kaduna (Ishaku, 2021). In addition, Adeola Akinremi, the feature editor of *ThisDay*, among others, received a death threat through email from Boko Haram in July 2015. Boko Haram has relied heavily on journalists' reports in the majority of its attacks on media outlets. This may be the cause of Galtung's (1965) observation that while war is reported in the media, peace journalism reveals the causes and dynamics of conflicts. He urged reporters to hear from all sides, investigate hidden objectives, and spotlight peace projects and ideas from anywhere at any time, as it is essential (Demarest & Langer, 2021).

Below are some excerpts from some Nigerian National Dailies. Yar'Adua and Aondover (2020) used it to analyse both peace journalism and war journalism based on Jayakumar's (2014) 'peace journalism and Boko Haram'.

A report from the *Nigerian Pilot* of Thursday, June 2, 2016:

Lai Mohammed Blames Boko Haram for Tomato Scarcity

Tomato shortages in the nation are allegedly caused by the terrorist rebel group Boko Haram, according to Minister of Information and Culture Lai Mohammed. The Minister claimed during an interview with Channels Television that the level of instability in the Northeast had driven farmers to leave the area. Mohammed's claim is at odds with that of Nigeria's agriculture minister, Chief Audu Ogbe, who singled out "Tuta Absoluta"—a pest so harmful to the red crop that it has been dubbed "tomato ebola"—as the cause of the current tomato shortage. Mohammed added, "When people discuss tomato prices, they often overlook the fact that the Boko Haram insurgency has caused us to lose two years' worth of harvest. This has a direct impact on tomato prices today". The majority of individuals riding okadas (motorcycles) in Lagos are those who would have worked on farms to manufacture consumable goods. "Do you farm where there is war?" the Minister asked, attributing the lack of tomatoes to insurgency. Two crop seasons are gone for us. (On page five. A Saturday, December 12, 2015, *Daily Trust* report).

Boko Haram Kills 7, Abducted Dozens in Borno Attack

In a new terrorist attack on a hamlet in Borno State, at least seven people were killed, and dozens of civilians were kidnapped, according to a local vigilante. After 11 PM on Thursday, while some residents were asleep, Boko Haram militants raided the remote community of Kamuya in the Biu local government area and kidnapped dozens of girls while killing seven others. According to Bukar Dili, a local vigilante in Biu town, the militants entirely burned the community down. At least five individuals were killed when they arrived in two SUVs and some motorcycles and began shooting randomly. At the same time, numerous young females were forcibly dragged away; it is unknown where they are today. According to Muhammed Yamutta, a different member of the Civilian JTF, the militants killed seven persons and kidnapped dozens of civilians.

As a result, several empirical questions in the literature have been linked to the Northeast as Nigeria's tomato food basket. Why has the fight been going on for more than five years yet the shortage just started? Is the Minister not only urging Nigerians to identify Boko Haram with their suffering? According to the second story, did *Daily Trust* get in touch with Boko Haram militants to learn why the incident happened? If the insurgents fully burned down the village, will the same story also claim that they killed seven individuals and kidnapped numerous villagers?

The aforementioned stories will be examined based on whether Nigerian peace journalism or war journalism was used, as well as how each strategy and angle affected the Boko Haram-related problems. When it comes to reporting on the Boko Haram insurgency, three things jump out, including propaganda, the "us-and-them" mentality, and the glaring absence of peace initiatives. These three elements can easily be thought of as the three devoted servants of war journalism. War journalism is the primary force behind the long-running, deadly conflict in the Northeast. It is the gasoline that keeps wars going. War journalism, according to Jayakumar (2014), is journalism that is centred on war and promotes the presentation that:

x.   It is primarily focused on violence, projects the conflict as a two-party, one-goal deal, restricts itself to a small space and time, and exclusively examines cause and effect in the conflict field.

xi. Reduce the struggle to obscurity by focusing exclusively on its outward, observable repercussions. The emphasis is on "we versus them" rhetoric, and Boko Haram is viewed as the issue and as the enemy.

xii. It is largely reactive in that it waits for hostility to break out before acting or speaking.

xiii. It is propaganda-focused, aiming only to reveal lies while aiding in the concealment of faults.

xiv. By emphasising "their" violence and "our" misery, labelling "them" as evildoers, and concentrating primarily on the elites' sector of society and spokespersons, it leans towards the elite.

xv. It is slanted toward victory; specifically, it views peace and a cease-fire as a victory while hiding peace attempts that have already been made before victory is at hand. It gives up on a war once it has stopped focusing on the core problem that needs to be resolved and only returns if the conflict flares up once more.

Therefore, what war media do is employ captives with strong voices to create unwarranted hype while reporting, causing everyone to say, "not anymore". But that's all they do. There is a sharp reduction in concerns about the violence after it has ended or faded from public memory, but little or nothing is done to understand its causes. As a result, there is a sort of bandage left on the wound, with little thought given to preventing future conflicts (Yar'Adua & Aondover, 2020).

Instead of focusing on the "winner-versus-loser issue", peace journalism goes straight to the source of the conflict. It stimulates the investigation of the foundations and context of conflict development and shows conflict from a realistic standpoint. The 'we versus them' issue is avoided by outlining the causes and opportunities for all parties concerned.

Challenges of Peace Journalism in Nigeria

In relation to peace journalism, many obstacles are seriously impeding professionalism in the Northeast (Yar'Adua & Aondover, 2020). Some of them are:

a) *Disclosing sources of information:* Truth and balance are the journalists' masters; neither the government nor Boko Haram is their master. Conflict reporting in the Northeast is hampered by the need to disclose the information's source. It was made abundantly clear that the government intended to use Ahmad Salkida, a journalist who covers Boko Haram, as an entry point to locate Boko Haram members when he was detained by the DSS at Nnamdi Azikiwe International Airport on September 5, 2016, according to a report in the *Daily Trust* and *Vanguard* Newspapers.

b) *Practical knowledge:* How many journalists actually understand how peace journalism works? While many people struggle to discern between peace journalism and traditional journalism, some may be fortunate enough to understand the rudimentary definition of peace journalism. So, how can they practice it if they lack the necessary knowledge?

c) *Poor remuneration:* A journalist will not take his profession seriously if he is not well paid. The time required to cover the crisis in the Northeast will not be sacrificed by him. Many journalists departed the Northeast when the conflict intensified and never came back. It's sad that many media outlets still owe writers money in salary arrears despite the professional expectation that journalists are supposed to refuse any type of inducement.

d) *Lack of professionalism:* This is one main cause of Boko Haram's attacks on some journalists and media organisations; they think these people have forgotten what professional conduct really means. The majority of Nigerian journalists, in contrast to other professions, disregard their codes of conduct and lack entry requirements for practice. Anyone who can write can claim to be a journalist. Sensationalism and anti-peace journalism are undermining the professional profile of many Nigerian newspapers. The gap between journalistic practice and school curricula needs to be filled in order to give Nigerian journalism practice its lost prestige. It becomes important to investigate the current codes of conduct in order to gradually make it impossible for charlatans to practice. A fair compensation package that is comparable to other professions should be in place.

Journalists as Perpetrators of Conflicts

News media and journalists have the potential to incite conflict. That is why ethical reporting is necessary. Vukasovich (2012) for instance, demonstrates that Radio Milles Collines in Rwanda instigated the 1994 genocide by using hate rhetoric and analogies. Similar to this, between 1995 and 1999, slanted reporting by Serbian official media contributed to the escalation of the Balkan hostilities.

In any unstable state, misinformation may fuel xenophobia, ethnic hatred, class conflict, and violent conflict. It is now well-established that ineffective journalism and politicised news management can do this. The aforementioned highlights the importance of responsible reporting and the consequent necessity for it, particularly in Africa, where Ubuntu journalism should be characterised by Afrocentric principles. This is significant because African knowledge and value systems should inform journalism in Africa.

Post-Conflict Peace-Building Process

Once a conflict has broken out, it is crucial to implement post-conflict peace-building processes in order to promote societal advancement. There are numerous stakeholders in this. In this aspect, journalists are crucial to the spread of information. Peace journalism gives violent incidents that would otherwise be reported on a daily basis new context, an appreciation of their underlying causes, and the ability to look for and analyse potential solutions. Orgeret and Tayeebwa (2016, p. 13) added that "post-conflict peace-building is a long-term process and is complex in nature, with the ultimate goal being to reconcile security development and justice". Some post-conflict peace-building techniques that journalists should use are as follows:

a)   Accountability;

b)   Aggressive philosophy of investigative journalism;

c)   Use of suitable skills to expose those responsible for human rights abuse;

d)   Lack of tolerance for military business mafias;

e) Zero acceptance of corruption;

f) Fair reporting on human insecurity;

g) Vandalism against the environment;

h) Covering those who abhor violence in news stories;

i) Not pointing the finger at any one race or continually referring to combatants as belonging to a particular race;

j) Reporting on the conflict's most fundamental causes;

k) Using language that brings people together rather than dividing them;

l) Positive imagery is employed in clause; and

m) Use of language that stresses the advantages of peace, such as growth and stability of the economy.

Conventional Strategies for Reporting Conflict

Shinar (2007, p. 200) proposed the following in focusing on the traditional methods of reporting conflict in response to "event-driven" war reporting that relies heavily on official sources:

1. Examining the settings and backgrounds that led to conflict and outlining the reasons behind each side's choices in order to show conflict in a transparent and realistic manner to the audience;

2. Giving voice to the opinions of all opposition groups;

3. Proposing innovative solutions for development, peacekeeping, and conflict resolution;

4. Disclose excesses perpetrated by and pain inflicted upon people of all parties, as well as expose lies, cover-up attempts, and offenders on all sides; and

5. Following post-war events and stories of peace.

Lessons from American versus Chinese Ways of Resolving Conflict

Americans and the Chinese have been observed to adopt a variety of dispute resolution techniques, including integration, insisting on one's own solution, compromising, surrendering to authority, avoiding passive resistance, severing the relationship, and a third-party method. In general, American participants were more inclined than Chinese participants to engage in conflict. However, because they are influenced by American and Chinese cultures, respectively, both strategies have value.

Chin et al in Chiakaan et al. (2023), stated that Chinese conflict resolution and reporting practices have their roots in Yijing, a Chinese philosophy based on the harmony of Ying and Yang and the acceptance of authority. Chinese mental programming's core cognitive mode is embodied by the Ying-Yang harmony. They stated that "Two partially conflicting yet complementary ideas or components (i.e. Ying and Yang) co-exist and are co-dependent in everything and interact with each other forever in a dynamic, contingent, and artistic manner". The employment of situation-specific and culturally specific conflict resolution strategies is influenced by different motivations. According to recent research, conflict resolution strategies that are grounded in people's cultural, social, and historical realities tend to be more successful.

As a result, traditional conflict resolution techniques like integrating, dominating, obliging, avoiding, and compromising, as suggested by Rahim and Bonoma (1979), can only make sense when taking into account people's socio-cultural realities. This is in line with other research which discovered that cultural background influences people's preferences for conflict management techniques. For example, Tang and Kirkbride (2018) found that British executives favoured more assertive tactics like engaging in competition and cooperation, while Chinese and Hong Kong government executives favoured less assertive tactics like avoidance and compromising.

Cheng et al. (2008) discovered that American managers favoured direct or solution-driven approaches, whereas Chinese managers tended to use more passive conflict-handling strategies like avoidance. The indications are that the key forces behind the American method of conflict resolution are personal force of reason and active logical examination. This relates to the ratio decidendi and obiter dictum-based American binary system of legal analysis that underlies decisions made by American courts. In the American legal system, ratio decidendi refers to a judge's unique interpretation of the law, whereas obiter dictum refers to the court's binding decision, signified by the word "we" and used by inferior courts. This one uses the pronoun "I" and is compelling, but lower courts cannot use it because it is not binding. It makes sense that the American approach to promoting peace and, by extension, peace journalism, is influenced by the same perspective.

Chinese participants (from Taiwan and Mainland China) employed more obliging and avoiding tactics than American participants, according to Yuan (2010), who also found that American participants exhibited a higher degree of dominating style than their Japanese and Korean counterparts. Consequently, improving conflict resolution involves prioritising social and cultural aspects. In this case, the proverb "one size does not fit all" does not apply.

The narrative demonstrates how Indigenous Knolwedge Systems (IKS) was used to settle a cow ownership issue between a traditional Chief and Hare.

There is no bull for the Hare. He sends his cow to the King, who agrees to let his bull fertilise Hare's cow since he wants it to be fertilised. Finally, Hare's cow becomes pregnant and gives birth to a healthy calf. It is allegedly the King's. When Hare sends a petition, it becomes a legal matter. On the day of the trial, Hare arrives late on purpose. Hare came late to the trial and when judges inquire as to why he was late, Hare asserts "seriously" and "innocently" that his father's bull, which was giving birth to a young calf, was the reason for his delay. The judges laughed off Hare, asking whether he was crazy. How long ago did a bull give birth? They asked this because they were curious. The lawsuit was won by Hare.

Media and Conflict Reporting in Nigeria

Data gathered at the Johns Hopkins University School of Advanced International Studies (SAIS) shows that between 1998 and 2014, over 29,600 people died in over 2,300 incidents in Nigeria, indicating a wide range of ethnic, religious, political, and economic tensions in significant segments of the nation's polity. As a result, every round of bloody fighting in any part of Nigeria exacerbates emotions of animosity throughout the country, makes the country poorer, and damages its reputation. The growing process is completely stopped, and long-standing ties are broken. The country and its citizens suffer collectively when millions of people are moved within their own borders (Pate & Dauda, 2017).

There has long been debate on the role of the media in times of conflict. The media has both explicitly stated and vague responsibilities as the watchdog and the fourth estate of the realm. In a multicultural and multiethnic society, one of the most fiercely contested subjects is how the media should handle conflict situations. In every culture where the population is diverse, it is imperative that the media foster amicable relations between individuals and groups with many varied and dynamic cultural identities. But in Nigeria, differences tend to exacerbate rifts, and it has been discovered that the media contributes to these splits.

As observed by Lynch and McGoldrick (2005) the media's involvement in conflicts around the world has not been particularly outstanding, which is partly due to the fact that traditional journalism practice is a victim of conflict. Galtung (2000) stated that modern journalism programmes even teach aspiring journalists that conflict is a standout feature of news. Unsurprisingly, this has an impact on how journalists behave when carrying out their roles as reporters or editors.

Cheng et al. (2008) turned to history to remind themselves that propaganda for wars and conflicts has frequently been done through the news media. They recall instances in which the media assisted in advancing Allied objectives during World War 1. They continue by pointing out that even in conflicts like those in Rwanda and the former Yugoslavia, local media had a significant part in promoting violence while the western media, despite their widespread presence, were powerless to change the trajectory of the developing conflict.

There are numerous well-known instances where the media is blamed for escalating hostilities around the globe. For example, radio was used in Rwanda to prepare the stage for genocide. Prior to the civil war in Serbia, ethnic tensions were stoked on television. Several contemporary opponents of the US war in Iraq contend that if the elite media had not supported President George W. Bush, it would have been difficult for the U.S. to invade Iraq. Additionally, the media in the former Soviet Republic of Georgia intensified territorial disputes. In Thailand, the media was cited as the primary source of motivation for the "Red Shirt" demonstrators during a three-month struggle that culminated in violence in 2011. Social media was found to be the primary cause of the catastrophic conflicts in the Middle East, despite the fact that it was commonly believed to be an indication of the approach of good government.

Cheng et al (2008) add that researchers have found that journalists are taught to create news within a "story" or narrative form that uses an antagonist going up against a protagonist, elements of dramatic tension, within a plot with the predictable elements of "a beginning, middle, and end". This format influences news in the prevailing cultural narratives that support the essentialist notion of a simple, clean battle against a wicked enemy while enticing adversaries to push perceived advantages, no matter how little.

The first casualty in any conflict situation, according to Pate and Dauda (2017), is frequently the manner in which the conflict players communicate with one another. Perhaps this explains why "breakdown in communication" is a common term used to describe conflict. Ordinary statements made by the actors are interpreted in the context of the disagreement, which could escalate the issue. On the basis of what they say and how they say it, it is therefore safe to argue that when third parties like the media incorrectly intervene, they can easily contribute to the situation escalating. The public views the media as the forerunner of an exact, factual, and true perspective on events, which accounts for people's reliance on them. As a result, it may be simple for the media to play a bad role in conflicts. Pate (2009) expressed the same viewpoint when he said that:

The employment of explosive, false, and provocative headlines by the media to boost readership is one of its problems. He claims that in a society that is already polarized and hostile, the media demonizes particular ethnic, religious, or political groups and employs cartoons to disparage a community, organisation, or individual. Above all, the media uses fictitious images in its stories; it can be objectively prejudiced and overtly unrepresentative of specific groups, people, or communities (p. 9).

In a dispute, antagonists and protagonists typically compete for media attention in an effort to sway public opinion and, eventually, public policy. This is accomplished through the media's ability to shape agendas and frames of thought. Discussions about the role of the mass media in society, particularly during campaigns, have long acknowledged the agenda-setting aspect. This could be the reason why Cohen (1963) claimed that while the media may not always be successful in influencing public opinion, it is astoundingly successful in influencing the opinions of its audience.

However, attempts have been made to analyse the media's coverage of topics related to diversity and violence in Nigeria and Africa (Pate, 2010). He observed that intergroup conflicts are primarily covered outside of fundamental sociological, economic, political, and other contexts; and the media creates negative preconceptions about groups and individuals through selective reporting.

Chapter Eight
Conflict Reporting in Journalism

Conflict occurs when two hostile or opposed forces, ideas, or elements collide. It happens at all levels of human contact, including in organisations, institutions, and private settings. At various levels, these conflicts are typically reported as normal and, unless they have an unusual quality, are rarely reported. In the local media, they are typically covered as crimes or as human-interest stories when they are reported. This chapter examines intra-national conflict in the context of peace journalism. Countries which have or are witnessing conflict like Northern Ireland, Lebanon, Sri Lanka, Sierra Leone, Liberia, Nicaragua, and Colombia, may have a generation of those who grew up believing that conflict was the norm. These were mostly intra-national conflicts. However, it was sometimes evident that outside interests were also involved, including those in the Middle East, the Falklands/Malvinas War of 1982 and the Wars in Iraq and Afghanistan. These conflicts serve as illustrations of wars with international ramifications.

All conflicts, to varied degrees, tend to put the peace in a group, an area, a country, or even the world at risk. Understanding conflict's nature and character is necessary for dealing with it, which necessitates recognising the key issues at hand and using the right strategies. Thus, attention must be paid to the origins, nature, and dynamics of conflict. The resolution of conflicts is a significant step in that direction, despite the claim that it is simply a "minimalist requirement" for the establishment of peace. Attempts at definitions that provide a context for comprehending the phenomenon will result from a more focused thought on conflict.

Perspectives on Conflict

Adaja (2012) characterised conflict more than 50 years ago as a fight over ideals and claims to limited position, power, and resources in which the opponents' goals are to neutralise, harm, and eliminate the other. Adaja (2012) established that conflict is a relationship between two or more parties who think their aims are at odds with one another. Conflict is the irreconcilable wants, different demands, contradicting wishes, competing ideas or divergent interests which cause interpersonal antagonism and, at times, aggressive confrontations. The resolution is defined as the settlement or avoidance of disagreements between individuals or groups of individuals through solutions that refrain from violence.

The Heidelberg Institute for International Conflict Research in 2005 defined conflict as:

The conflict between, at least, two parties (organized groups, states, groups of states, organizations) that is committed to pursuing its interests and winning its cases over the course of time and size regarding national ideals (p. 2).

Regardless of the variety of definitions, there is always a common thread that contains elements of dispute, whether it is on issues of principle, perception, policy, ideology, culture, or expectation. Beyond this, the fact that conflict arises and develops through stages is a crucial component in discussions of conflict. It is a cycle that is capable of being split up into different stages.

Therefore, the term conflict has two things: relationships and the reality that, as opposed to objective facts, people's views about goals are the source of conflict. In a relationship, conflict arises when people think that their goals cannot be fulfilled at the same time or when they see a difference in their needs, values, and interests (latent conflict). When people deliberately use their power to undermine, neutralise, or destroy one another in an attempt to safeguard or advance their interests in the relationship (manifest conflict), there is conflict.

Phases of Conflicts

Brahm in Adaja (2012) depicts a typical conflict progression curve that he divides into seven stages or phases. They consist of the:

a)   Latent conflict stage;

b)   Conflict emergence stage;

c)   Conflict escalation stage;

d)   Stalemate stage;

e)   De-escalation/negotiation stage;

f)   Dispute/settlement stage; and

g)   Post-conflict peace-building stage.

Noll (2000) distinguishes five stages of conflict escalation, each with distinct traits and causes. According to his theory, parties often exhibit behaviours that indicate a step backwards due to stress as a conflict progresses through several phases. Noll views the first phase, in which people cooperatively seek unbiased solutions, as a natural aspect of everyday life. The conflict worsens if a resolution is not found at this time, particularly if one of the participants is adamantly clinging to their own viewpoint. In the second phase, the parties alternate between cooperating and competing, and each one makes every effort to avoid displaying any signs of weakness. Therefore, both sides worry that there will be no room for a compromise in the third phase.

The conversation turns hostile. Each party is aware of the perspectives of the other when the conflict enters its fourth stage, but they are no longer able to take them into account. If this fight is not stopped, it becomes even more intense. The fifth and final phase, according to Noll, is when the fight takes on mythical proportions and the parties occasionally harbour omnipotence delusions.

Triangle and Levels of Conflict Analysis

One of the pioneers of peace and conflict studies, Galtung (1996), created a conflict triangle model to illustrate how conflicts are structured. A conflict, according to him, is made up of behaviour (B), assumptions and attitudes (A), and a contradiction (C). While A and C are latent, the B-component is manifest (behaviour is, by definition, observable). Conflict thus takes the shape of a triangle, and the flows and interactions between the triangle's three sides serve to show how dynamic conflicts are. Galtung believes that because conflict has its own lifetime, it is almost biological (Pate & Jibril, 2024).

We see a progressive rise in conflict from a controllable level to a crescendo, where it effectively falls out of control, when we examine the many definitions and stages and progression of conflict as enunciated by various experts. The greatest outcome that can be anticipated at this point is that the parties attempt to "pick up the pieces" and return to the point where the conflict started.

According to Anstey in Aondover et al. (2024), the three conflict analysis frameworks of Noll's five stages, Brahm's seven stages, and Galtung's triangle can be combined to create the hidden and manifest conflict levels of analysis. The first two phases of latent conflict and conflict emergence from Kriesberg, as well as Galtung's attitude (A) and contradictions (C) parts of the conflict triangle, are all included in the latent level. During the third stage, the parties alternate between cooperating and contending. The subsequent phases of the other models, as well as Galtung's behaviour (B) element, would be included in the manifest conflict level. Understanding how media can meaningfully contribute to the pursuit of peace is made easier by recognising the latent/manifest distinction.

The idea put forward here is that resolution is relatively simpler to achieve when conflict is faced at the point where managing it is least difficult and complicated, when emotions are not at their peak, and when attitudes and contradictions are not consolidated into hard-to-break behaviours. Ideas still have a chance of being put forth and taken into consideration at Galtung's "attitude" and "contradiction" levels, where they have a better chance of averting acts of violence or other outward conflict (Aondover et al., 2024).

It is crucial that these two levels of conflict are separated in this way. Conflict of the manifest kind is what we read about most frequently when it occurs. Latent conflict frequently goes unnoticed since it isn't noticeable enough to draw attention. It operates under the radar and is not acknowledged or valued for what it truly is. Manifest conflict, on the other hand, is what creates "good" news and "excellent" reporting. Therefore, manifest and latent conflict reporting require deeper level of understanding and analysis.

Conflict and Manifest Conflict Reporting

Pate and Jibril (2024) observed that the first journalism course in any curriculum will cover the elements of newsworthiness. Conflict, oddity, closeness, size, significance, and human interest are a few of these. Many of these elements are common in wars. Manifest conflict is the main feature of war because of the high death rates, conflicts are very interesting to reporters. News stories that make people say "wow!" include bombings that result in the deaths of over 350 people. Furthermore, because of their physical proximity or shared cultural or religious beliefs, different segments of the global audience often identify with one or both of the opposing sides, meeting the proximity requirement. When combined, this will produce some human interest that the reporter can address. As a result, journalists are drawn to war, which is unquestionably the highest form of manifest conflict (Garba & Aondover, 2023).

The Middle East's territorial claims, Rwanda's genocide aftermath, South Africa's and some European countries' xenophobic reactions, the actions of occupation forces in Iraq and Afghanistan, insurgencies in Sri Lanka, and civil wars in Nigeria, Sierra Leone, Liberia, and Ivory Coast are all subject to journalists with manifest conflict. All of these situations provide journalists with easily reportable information. When covering conflicts, news is seen as a product that must be marketed. As long as news is viewed as a commodity, especially by the mainstream media, obviously, conflictual reporting will be the most enticing type of reporting (Aondover et al., 2024). It will be challenging to persuade journalists to concentrate on events that have not yet reached the brink of explosion as their primary means of producing income for the media. Such occasions would need to be magnificent!

Latent Conflict Reporting: The Nigeria Niger-Delta Crisis

Latent conflict rarely attracts attention, almost invariably. However, it is at this level that those whose interests are being taken into account and reported on can manage conflict most effectively. Manifest conflict is frequently at the forefront of the minds of journalists and academics that support peace journalism. It is safe to argue that applying peace journalism to latent conflict reporting will aid in averting the inferno that manifests conflict frequently represents (Aondover & Abba, 2017). Other academics have, in fact, drawn attention to the possibility of such early action in interstate conflicts. According to Karl Deutsch, "continuing hostile attention in the mass media may tend to harden public opinion to such a degree as to ultimately destroy the freedom of choice of the national government concerned".

As a result, he proposed "an early warning system" to track the amount of media attention given to a conflict area or an enemy nation. His goal was to "quantitatively assess the relative proportions of attention given to different interstate conflicts and issues in the overall news flow, the amount to which leaders retain or overlook these, and the extent to which they have cumulative consequences". Later, Cees Hamelink proposed the creation of an International Media Alert System (IMAS) to keep track on media coverage in crisis zones. This system would give "early warning" of where and when the media creates an environment conducive to crimes against humanity and starts to incite people to commit murder.

Latent conflict is essentially an instance of people, groups, or nations expressing disagreements over values or concepts. At this point, protagonists are most likely to listen to one another and communicate well. At this stage, the chances of success are higher for negotiation and mediation. One of the biggest barriers to discussion that could result in peace is the introduction of violence at the upper (manifest) level. It is even possible that one side does not recognise a problem while it is at the latent conflict stage. This is comparable to what happens in interpersonal social connection or interaction (Garba & Aondover, 2023).

The Niger-Delta region of Nigeria comprises the nine states of Abia, AkwaIbom, Bayelsa, Cross River, Delta, Edo, Imo, Ondo, and Rivers. This country is made up of 36 states and the Federal Capital Territory (FCT). Over 60% of the country's Gross Domestic Product (GDP) comes from oil and gas produced in this region. Although the region provides what has become the nation's economic sustenance, the indigenous population of the region has suffered deprivation and adequate access to the dividends of the resources they produce.

According to Emeka in Nwagbara et al., (2018) the conflict in the Niger-Delta region can be linked to the government's and the oil industry's pervasive neglect and marginalisation of important human development, infrastructure, and the provision of fundamental social amenities. Despite being surrounded by wealth, the locals in this area live in poverty. They have observed as oil has been produced from their land and the money made from it has been utilised to develop areas of the country far away from where they live. As (small-scale) fishermen, the majority of these locals rely on the streams' waters for their livelihood.

Oil corporations began and continued the exploration of oil at a time when environmental damage from spills was widespread, and the companies either took very little action or did nothing to stop it. Poverty increased, fishing activity was negatively impacted, and the water was polluted. Malnutrition, water-borne illnesses, and inadequate sanitation all contributed to a rise in mortality among the general populace. Emeka observed that one ethnic group, the Ogoni, in particular, suffered from privation and poverty as their land was abused and their source of subsistence was badly jeopardised. Ngoro in Nwagbara et al. (2018), captured it thus:

A concrete example is the Ogoni community in Rivers state's Niger-Delta, whose cause is being led by the Movement for the Survival of Ogoni People (MOSOP) and former human rights advocate Ken Saro-Wiwa. They noted, along with other communities in the Niger-Delta region, that their water was poisoned, their atmosphere was polluted, and their fields had been ravaged and ruined. this as a result of the local oil corporations' operations (p. 1).

The Ogoni people have long protested to officials at all levels of government about the hardship they are going through, including the absence of infrastructure facilities in their towns like electricity, drinkable water, and access to roads. However, nobody was interested in hearing. Slowly, the feeling of deprivation turned into frustration, which then turned into wrath. This process took a long time. By November 1999, the Ogoni people were incensed. Nwagbara et al. (2018), note that they had submitted the Federal Government of Nigeria a bill of rights requesting political independence that would ensure political control and the utilisation of Ogoni economic resources for Ogoni development and the authority to stop the continuing degradation of the Ogoni environment and ecology.

The Ogonis had insisted on remediation measures at this point. All they wanted was for their situation to change, but no one paid serious attention to them. Government at all levels did not have major conversations with them. Violence became the recourse, starting with intra-community killings. The Ogoni conflict grew to be very serious. Other minority groups were drawn to it and supported the call for resource control. This eventually resulted in what is now known as the Niger-Delta crisis, which has taken numerous lives and increased the level of insecurity throughout the nation.

Obviously, this account does not fully capture the complexity of the Niger-Delta issue. However, the purpose of this story is to demonstrate how latent conflict can become more serious and violent if ignored. When individuals first began to complain about the state of the environment, the government paid little attention. The murders, maiming, and abductions could have been stopped if they had. Evidently, they did not adequately express or sustain their worries in ways that could get the attention they merited. By engaging at the point where discussion would still have been a possibility, peace journalism could have achieved this. Therefore, the Niger-Delta example serves as a metaphor for problems around the globe that might have been averted if necessary action had taken place at the right (latent) stage of the conflict.

To however claim that the media alone could have been a sufficient deterrent to the growth of the crises in the Niger-Delta or other analogous problem regions throughout the world would be overstating the case. It may still be argued, though, that the media can serve as a useful conversation starter. The majority of disputes are mostly local in nature, especially when they are latent. The question would be how national and international media intervene in a strictly local environment. This is a question that highlights the need for preventive peace journalism to begin at the local level. If the local media engages at the proper level, externality need not be a requirement for peace-building.

This duty of encouraging discussion between the parties should be assumed by the local print and broadcast media that are in the conflict zone. They may accomplish this not simply by re-enacting the "incident", but also by conducting research, gathering important information, and presenting it to the persons involved for consideration. Because they are local, the media are familiar with the problems and all of its intricacies. As a result, individuals are able to engage and persist in the pursuit of solutions.

The idea of "localised" journalism is not new. The community journalism that was encouraged in the 1970s and 1980s is focused locally while yet providing professional coverage. It emphasises local neighbourhoods and, while covering events outside emphasises the impacts those events have on the neighbourhood. Similarly, civic journalism, which started to spread across the U.S. in the 1990s, was viewed as "essential to the reconstruction of public life" by its proponents.

Chapter Nine
Artificial Intelligence and Algorithmic Journalism

Artificial Intelligence (AI) has already been utilised in journalism for sometime. The use of AI in journalism is now more widespread and varied in its applications. Journalism, which is the communication of facts about current events, is an area that is subject to an increasing amount of AI activity. The increase is attributed to the large volume of news data available electronically and the urgency of real-time online journalism. The application of AI technologies to simulate human cognition in the analysis, interpretation, and comprehension of complex data is a natural fit for the needs of journalism. In terms of providing a competitive angle for this book, AI in journalism is expected to have a very high impact, hence making it a relevant topic.

Therefore, the practice of employing software to generate news articles or news story pieces is known as automated journalism, sometimes known as algorithmic journalism. With the availability of big data and statistical software, automated journalism is becoming increasingly popular. This process involves the identification of a set of data, for example sports statistics or election results, and the input of this data into a software program. This data is then converted into a news story by using the software to apply a prewritten set of rules and algorithms to make decisions about what content should be included (AlQadi, 2024). This decision-making process is what sets AI apart from other types of software that have been used to assist with journalism in the past. The applications of AI in journalism streamline workflows, improve efficiency, and enable journalists to produce high-quality, data-driven content more effectively. However, ethical considerations, such as bias in algorithms and job displacement, must be addressed to ensure responsible and equitable AI implementation in journalism.

Also, ChatGPT, a version of GPT-3, which OpenAI has made publicly available with the intention of being used to develop conversational agents or chatbots. A chatbot is a computer program that conducts a conversation with users typically using auditory or textual methods. They are designed to simulate how a human would behave as a conversational partner (Bdoor & Habes, 2024). The programme functioned by ChatGPT is significantly different from the AI journalism tools that have come before it – primarily in terms of its usability. For example, there have been tools created to automatically generate news stories from structured data using natural language generation, but to this date, none of these have been widely adopted by journalists or media outlets. This is largely because they aren't good enough. Currently, a human journalist is going to do a better job of writing a news story than a computer program because journalists are able to use high-quality data and a wide array of industry knowledge to write stories that are clear, relevant, and interesting (Bdoor & Habes, 2024).

The stories that can be created by previous AI journalism tools are often factually inaccurate, poorly structured, and uninteresting. So, they are not 'better' than what human journalists can produce (Zafrullah et al., 2024). This is where the potential impact lies. OpenAI's decision to create ChatGPT as a conversational AI is a clear indication that the goal behind GPT-3 is to develop something that is 'better' than a human journalist at producing news content from both a reader engagement perspective and from an informational integrity perspective. OpenAI believes that the conversational capabilities that are smoke-screened by the AI's current lack of industry knowledge can be built on, and when this is achieved, it will produce a tool that is better than anything that currently exists in the form of a human journalist.

These advances have had some degree of impact on almost all of society's institutions, journalism not being an exception. From its onset, it has been widely understood that the diffusion of new technologies into the workplace can be obtained either through a process of adaptation in which the new technology is in some way made to conform to the existing work practices or through a process of reconfiguration where the new technology is used as a tool to change the work practice into a new form (Zafrullah et al., 2024). An example of such reconfiguration is the impact of the internet on print journalism. In this case, the internet was not used as a tool to make the journalist write news stories in the same way but rather provided a new medium for the dissemination of information and opened up many new employment areas in online journalism, and it had a dramatic effect on the economic sustainability of print journalism.

Overall, ChatGPT can complement traditional journalism practices by enhancing productivity, engaging audiences, and providing innovative ways to deliver news content. However, ethical considerations, such as transparency about the use of AI and safeguarding against biases, are essential to ensure responsible and ethical journalism.

Throughout history, technology has always had an impact on the media industry. The last 10 years have witnessed an extraordinarily significant transformation in the field of journalism, with many of its fundamental concepts being redefined, despite the discipline's continued and tight relationship to technology improvements (Deuze & Witschge, 2018). This change was influenced by the advent of innovative, cutting-edge technologies like artificial intelligence and natural language generation. The way the journalism profession is practised has changed dramatically as a result of these advancements, particularly when considering how they affect the production and dissemination of news and create a plethora of new opportunities for news gathering and consumption.

As automation and computerisation have grown in popularity, journalism has also seen a surge in the replacement of mundane activities by technology. Many automated algorithms began to replace human workers in the workplace by taking on various tasks as artificial intelligence advanced over time (Aondover, 2019). From easier tasks like gathering basic data to more challenging ones like creating news articles entirely from scratch using modern algorithms, the complexity of these activities grew over time to the point were, at this point, every step of the news creation process may be automated (Van-Dalen, 2012). All of the aforementioned methods can be collectively referred to as "algorithmic journalism".

Thus, the term "algorithmic journalism" refers to the approach that the news industry has adopted as a result of recent technological developments. The technique of using software or algorithms to automatically generate news items without human input is known as "algorithmic journalism". There are instances when the terms algorithmic, computational, robotic, and automated journalism are used interchangeably. These ideas could also be broadly described as the application of data, algorithms, and social science expertise to improve journalism's accountability role (Hamilton & Turner, 2009).

While expanding the term can be highly helpful in comprehending all of its sides, it should be emphasised that doing so should be avoided because it makes it difficult to determine the precise focus of the subject matter. The term "computer-assisted reporting" (CAR) has been used since the emergence of digital technology to refer to any kind of digital assistance that journalists utilise in their job, including the use of personal computers for simple tasks like conducting online research. Okon (2021) makes an effort to differentiate between the two terms because of this, highlighting that, although algorithmic journalism still uses the term, CAR focuses more on the processing power of contemporary software than on the more commonplace uses of technology by journalists, such as data storage and access (Kurfi et al., 2021).

In order to evaluate the ways in which journalism has changed over the past ten years and to better comprehend the roots of this discussion, it is imperative that we look at the specific domains within the confines of the journalistic profession where algorithms and automation have had the most impact.

Areas of Application of Algorithmic Journalism

It should be noted that the use of algorithms in journalism may extend much beyond the areas that are included here. According to Okon (2021), the following ones seem to offer the most significant services:

1.   Automated content production;

2.   Data mining;

3.   News dissemination; and

4.   Content optimisation.

Automated content production

The automation of the news-creation process is one of the biggest and, thus, most controversial use of algorithmic technology in journalism. Globally, the field of journalism is viewed as having advanced very recently in this particular application, which is primarily composed of automated software and algorithms that can independently produce news articles.

One of the most well-known examples of early adoption for automated content creation is the "Quakebot" programme established by the Los Angeles Times in 2014. Its objective was to closely monitor U.S. Geological Survey data in an attempt to identify seismic activity, and then to prepare and disseminate clear reports on the findings (Okon, 2021). Since then, there has been a major advancement in automated content creation. As a result, some of the largest players in the industry, such as Forbes and The New York Times, routinely use algorithmic production for their material, and the final output is almost identical to human writing.

The technology that forms the basis for developments in automated content production is called natural language generation, or NLG for short. The notion of "natural language generation", which is "the automatic synthesis of text from digital structured data", was first used in relation to machine translation in the 1950s. Many industries have begun to use NLG in conjunction with artificial intelligence to further improve their services and goods as a result of its recent exponential rise. This tendency is not unique to the news media industry.

Advantages of Automated Content Production

The use of these technologies by the journalism industry appeared to have a number of advantages, such as a notable boost in productivity as a result of stories being published without the need for human intervention. Additionally, journalists were able to redefine their core competencies and enjoy greater creative freedom in their work as a result of computers taking over routine tasks and fulfilling some of their duties (Ali & Hassoun, 2019). The growing market demand for fast and accurate news reports seems to be amplifying the advantages of algorithmic news generation.

Disadvantage of Automated Content Production

The aforementioned benefit has, in turn, sparked a range of debates among those in the journalism business. The prospect that the automation process would make human employees in the field obsolete is the main topic of conversation among journalists and others working in the news industry as a whole. Many arguments have been made in the literature on this subject, and many employees have also expressed their opinions, arguing that the future of human journalists will be seriously threatened by the growing prominent role of algorithms in the newsroom. On the other end of the spectrum, a lot of studies seem to believe that those worries are mostly unjustified; pointing out that over time, algorithms and artificial intelligence will only improve journalistic practice rather than replace it.

However, it is undeniable that automated content creation plays a significant part in the news production process today, and scholars generally concur that automation will play a crucial part in the future of news organisations. The use of automated content production tools appears to be the only option to keep up with the continuously growing need for more news items as industry competitiveness increases. However, there is still uncertainty regarding how the industry will adjust to these new automation-related conditions, as employee displacement and a workforce reduction, in general, are indeed projected to occur as machines become more and more capable of taking the place of human workers in some particular tasks (Hamilton & Turner, 2009).

Data Mining

The so-called "data explosion" which refers to the ongoing growth of publicly accessible material on the internet, is one of the most notable features of the information era currently being experienced. According to Ali and Hassoun (2019), the size of the digital universe approximately doubles every 18 months. However, information should not be confused with data. Journalists are battling more than ever to sort through the complexity of available information in this ever-growing resource landscape, and this is where techniques like data mining start to become necessary.

Ali and Hassoun (2019) observed that data mining is the process of extracting meaningful information from a wider subset of data and is a key component of a bigger process known as knowledge discovery. The most obvious application of this technology in journalism is the extraction of specific information from large databases. Though primarily recognised as an example of automated content generation, the "Quakebot" scenario described above is also an excellent illustration of data mining, as the computer was able to recognise and extract information from a much larger dataset (all of the U.S. Geological

Survey's data). Chatboxes and other automated agent kinds have been extensively utilised in these procedures.

Beyond this more obvious use case, however, data mining technology can be applied to a multitude of other difficult jobs related to journalism. Algorithmic data mining is the only sensible way to handle so-called "Big Data" when datasets are too big for humans to comprehend because of things like their volume (terabytes to petabytes) or their velocity (being created in real time). Journalists utilise these kinds of data sets all the time, and data mining can help them uncover links between variables that were previously unknown but had high statistical significance. This can then allow them to test complex ideas and hypotheses (Deuze, 2003). When combined with automated content creation, data mining can be used to identify emerging social trends, automatically target specific audiences for whom the content would be more relevant, and open up new application areas similar to those seen in algorithmic journalism.

Arguments on Data Mining

The undeniable value of algorithmic mining, particularly in online environments with user interaction like social media, can occasionally be eclipsed by privacy concerns about user surveillance that may result in social discrimination. This kind of analysis of metadata can occasionally reveal information that is even more important than the uploaded item itself. Of course, just like with any tool, the purpose of using data mining software is just as crucial as any practical issues that might be present. For this reason, studies like the one mentioned above advocate for the democratisation of these processes by introducing regulations and more stringent democratic oversight. In addition to the foregoing, the accessibility issue also pertains to these sophisticated technologies. Similar to the introduction of algorithmic news production, the introduction of Big Data and the proper procedures necessary to analyse them have had a significant impact on the news industry, not only in terms of productivity but also in terms of the skills necessary to work in this new and rapidly changing environment of journalism.

Modern tools and specialised software should be available to news industry employees so they can completely utilise Big Data to enhance their reporting and information-gathering procedures and understand the intricate information concealed in sizable datasets. One argument, closely related to the problems with automated content production, holds that workers will need to take on more specialised tasks in order to compete in this more automated workplace.

Many of the points made regarding automated programs taking the place of human workers in content production also apply to algorithmic data mining, while there are some clear exceptions, such as the study of Big Data itself. Given that Big Data and related concepts are inherently incomprehensible for human processing and would remain unreachable without the assistance of algorithms, it seems that software agents in these scenarios merely function to enhance the competencies of contemporary journalists without posing a threat to the employment of human labour.

News Dissemination

A significant amount of everyday media consumption now occurs online; as a result, the manner in which news is disseminated becomes extremely crucial. The majority of internet users get their news content from three main sources: news aggregators, search engines, and social networking platforms. All of these digital intermediaries have one thing in common: to properly distribute material to their users, they heavily rely on automated systems and algorithms. These automatic news transmission technologies turned out to be a significant driving factor for journalism as news organisations began to use them more. This was because media businesses started to move their focus to online news and the introduction of more interactive elements (Hamilton & Turner, 2009).

The advantages of applying these innovations in the journalistic industry quickly became apparent. Specifically, news companies were able to automate and methodically distribute news on social media and other similar channels by utilising software agents referred to as "news bots". By improving the process of news dissemination and helping media organisations reach the widest audience possible, these applications can transmit news and information to a large audience, connect with users in a number of ways, and guarantee that the relevant content is highly visible (Deuze, 2003).

Criticism Regarding News Dissemination

Although not to the same degree as automated content development, controversy has also been noted in this area of application. Researchers have expressed concerns, in particular over the years, about the function of algorithmic news distribution technology as a "gatekeeper" of news, the accountability and objectivity of these programs, ethical issues surrounding algorithmic transparency and the part these agents play in the spread of false information. All of the aforementioned represent well-funded news distribution relating to criticism that has not yet been adequately handled (Ali & Hassoun, 2019).

Li et al. (2011), raise a significant point about the intermediation problem, specifically in relation to news gatekeeping. It is difficult to guarantee that news distribution will continue to be democratic in the future because it is projected that more than 70% of internet news traffic is being redirected by digital intermediaries. This raises a lot of concerns about how journalism will develop in the future, including concerns about quality decline and potential censorship problems that might potentially affect a very big segment of the public. The survival of the journalism industry will depend on maintaining open lines of communication and preventing outside parties from routinely elevating some views above others. It is difficult to evaluate the effectiveness of algorithms in this area because there is ultimately no accepted norm for humans acting as news censors.

Content Optimisation

Since some scholars have proposed working models for it even before the start of the twenty-first century, personalised content for particular recipients is not a new thing in the media industry. However, it wasn't until recently that advancements in algorithmic technology permitted news providers to target particular audiences on a big scale and provide personalised news experiences for them. This is a result of the internet's capacity to deliver suggestions and knowledge from all around the world in virtually real-time. These personalised news content services have proven to be quite helpful because they can save users' time by substantially reducing the amount of information that is not relevant to them and by only providing content on topics that they are interested in.

Search engines use automated ranking algorithms to return the most pertinent results for a user's search, and content optimisation for users typically operates in a similar way. Automated algorithms are used to provide tailored news articles and internet advertisements to particular consumers in a manner similar to this. As some firms use algorithms for activities like A/B testing story headlines in order to more accurately assess their efficacy, content optimisation using algorithmic technology has also been seen in various stages of the news production process. However, the main application of this technology has been to deliver personalised news information via automated agents like chatbots or customised newsfeeds. Compared to more conventional means of material consumption, these automated bots in particular have shown to be particularly effective at engaging audiences by offering more interactive and personalised examples of news and articles.

Problems of Content Optimisation

Technology is very important, however, there have been certain problems with its use that need to be fixed. First, over the years, a few personal concerns about content optimisation have been brought up. These worries are particularly connected to the way these algorithmic solutions work because the majority of content optimisation systems from media companies and other enterprises alike depend on the collection of personal data in order to perform their functions (Ghasemi et al., 2024).

The fact that people frequently overlook the personalisation these algorithms utilise exacerbates this problem. Because many users find it uncomfortable to think that they are "being watched" by automated programmes while they are online, even if those programmes are ultimately meant to provide them with more streamlined recommendations, many researchers, such as Sama (2024), have started to advocate for algorithmic transparency.

Another pertinent issue in this field of application is the content that is being conveyed. Scholars such as Zhong et al (2024) have observed that the continuous flow of tailored content could potentially harm the news ecosystem, as it is known to reduce users' access to a range of news sources and thus lead to partial information blindness. The phenomena known as "filter bubbles" gained popularity, while related theoretical ideas such as "news echo chambers" explained how consumers were continuously exposed to similar points of view.

The absence of diverse viewpoints in online environments is a significant criticism of news personalisation, as it often serves to reinforce the user's opinion on particular topics without providing counterarguments, or alternative viewpoints. While this phenomenon is not exclusive to these technologies, or the internet—it is also evident in other media—the way customised material is delivered online appears to be exacerbating this specific issue.

Algorithmic personalisation, therefore, both encloses users in their own "bubble" and keeps them from questioning their ideas while simultaneously catering to their requirements and creating a more delightful and adaptable experience. This argument calls into question the tailored news delivery paradigm because it may inadvertently lead to some grave consequences in the future, such as the dispersal of false information, or the potential splintering of the public's view.

Challenges and Future Implementation of Algorithmic Technology

Even while algorithmic technology has made great strides recently, there are still several challenges facing it. Most of them have to do with automated content production because it's an extremely complex and demanding field of application by nature. One of automated journalism's main disadvantages is its dependence on structured data. Topics cannot be handled without enough structured data being accessible for them, as modern algorithmic solutions mostly rely on structured data to build articles.

For this approach, since poor data quality would likely result in less accurate reporting, data quality is just as crucial as data availability. Although algorithms have become more adept at creating journalistic material and imitating human writing over time, there are still several critical areas in which computers still lag behind people, and experts do not believe that this scenario will improve any time soon (Ghasemi et al., 2024). The ability to make inferences, pose questions, and explain novel phenomena using the information presented are the major components of these skills.

These facts presently maintain a gap between news-writing algorithms and humans, no matter how successful automated journalism can be, especially in scenarios where the event's structure is repetitive, or predictable, such as sports events, or weather forecasts. More difficult to overcome than the technical issues could prove to be the editorial challenges posed by automated content development. It is expected of journalists to acquire the requisite "computational thinking" skills to mitigate any shortcomings the algorithms may display in that domain and work closely with these programmes to ensure the best outcome to overcome these challenges.

There are difficulties and restrictions with regard to other domains of application than automated content production. While algorithms are excellent at finding links between various variables when it comes to data mining, oftentimes their findings might be useless, or even result in incorrect conclusions. These erroneous findings may have been made for a variety of reasons, including faulty data, improper questions, and artificial intelligence techniques. This underlines the fact that regardless of how effective these tools may be, their proper application is still crucial and frequently necessitates adequate understanding on the part of media professionals in order to produce the desired outcomes in the context of journalistic research (Smyth, 2020).

Despite all of the examples given, algorithmic technology is still a very promising area for the profession's growth, and researchers are hopeful that automation and artificial intelligence will help journalists overcome some of the most difficult challenges facing modern journalism, such as the abundance of information and the associated credibility issues (Ali & Hassoun, 2019). As with nearly all other professions affected by automation, the introduction of more advanced news algorithms in the future is likely to cause some turbulence in the industry. However, it is widely believed that the potential that these programmes carry will help journalists to produce news at a faster pace, on a larger scale, and with fewer errors.

Scholars like Ali and Hassoun (2019) have remarked that as technology advances, algorithms can be used to cover events that would be financially unviable to cover in the present (such as particular sports with little turnout or interest) and to produce audio-visual reports in addition to text-based ones. By transforming raw data into engaging stories, autonomous programmes might be charged with "creating stories in locations where no one is writing stories", which has the potential to significantly extend the news writing landscape.

While these trends are undoubtedly advantageous for media plurality, the increase in news output and some of the issues with content distribution and optimisation that were raised earlier in the article could potentially compound into a different kind of problem. In particular, there is a serious danger of information overload in the media environment because the amount of material available will grow exponentially over time as a result of faster production and improved dissemination techniques. According to Smyth (2020), automated journalism will significantly increase the volume of news that is available, which will make it harder for consumers to identify the information that is most important to them. Future thinking should definitely take this perspective into account, particularly given how the spread of false information and fake news is likely to exacerbate the issue.

The development of a fully autonomous news system is another endeavour that may out to be quite promising. Such a system could combine different application areas like data mining, algorithmic content production, news dissemination, and optimisation in order to sort through information, write reports based on the collected data, and distribute the finished product to the right audiences, all without the need for human intervention (Ghasemi et al., 2024). Examples such as the one with "Quakebot" demonstrate that the idea can function in principle, even though putting this into practice will definitely be challenging. This is especially true for events that have a recurrent structure, like weather reports.

Chapter Ten
Global Journalistic Threats

The past ten years have seen a marked upsurge in violence and intimidation against journalists worldwide. Even today, too many journalists are dying in the line of duty. Risk and unpredictability are inherent in any dangerous situation (Dad & Khan, 2020). Local journalists working in countries plagued by authoritarian governments, war, organised crime, and corruption make up the great majority of those killed and kidnapped. Numerous journalists have been assassinated, kidnapped, harassed, attacked, or compromised. Most are independent contractors with little financing, little experience, and often no established media platform to completely support them (Dad & Khan, 2020).

Journalism and the media have undergone a dramatic transformation that has fundamentally altered how news is produced, consumed, and transmitted. The safety of journalists has been affected by these social and digital shifts. Since intimidation, vilification, and violence against journalists have repercussions for freedom of expression, democratic values, and public access to information generally. These threats also have an effect on society as a whole in addition to the targeted journalists. This chapter discusses the most important and recent threats to journalists around the world, as well as potential policy recommendations that could be made to ensure their safety and promote an environment that is supportive of accountability and free speech protection so that these threats can be reduced.

Media professionals face numerous risks, including but not limited to conflicts, civil unrest, hit squads, rogue militias, rape and other gender-based crimes, cyberbullying, emotional trauma, drug cartels, explosives and crossfire, natural disasters, and epidemics. Many news outlets, particularly in developing nations, lack the financial means to provide reporters with security-enhancing resources like encryption software, security training, legal assistance, flak jackets, and bodyguards. Even those employed by relatively wealthy Western news organisations are unaware of the vital training and other resources provided by NGOs, or private enterprises.

Mapping Threats to Journalists in the World

The threats that journalists confront around the world are evolving quickly and getting more complicated. For example, Reporters Without Borders (2019) discovered that the number of journalist fatalities in 2019 was "historically low". But upon closer inspection, it became clear that the decline in numbers was mostly due to fewer journalists being killed in conflict zones rather than more press freedom and safety for journalists. Attacks on journalists covering protests and large crowds have increased; since 2015, at least 10 journalists have been killed while reporting protests, according to the UNESCO Observatory of Killed Journalists (Smyth, 2020). According to UNESCO research, political rhetoric critical of the media has increased antagonism toward the press, which frequently manifests itself in attacks on specific journalists.

Although there are still risks associated with reporting in the field, there is a greater likelihood of attacks and violence against journalists covering terrorism, human rights violations, gang violence, state corruption, and criticism of public authorities. Journalists may also face violence because of their identity, which includes aspects of their gender, sexual orientation, colour, and membership in a minority group. Examples of women journalists being killed in Pakistan by their family members for refusing to give up a career in media, or so-called "honour killings," have been documented (Mushtaq, 2019). These situations demand an intersectional and contextual vision of safety. Those against female journalists who "violate the rules of gender inequalities and stereotypes" occur more frequently than attacks against men. Due to the topic of their stories, journalists covering "feminist problems" risk harassment, or legal repercussions.

Several journalists are arbitrarily detained around the world, either via the employment of restrictive legislation or extrajudicially. The number of unlawfully detained journalists worldwide increased by 12% in 2023 (Westlund et al., 2024). According to the Committee to Protect Journalists (CPJ), 248 journalists were imprisoned in 2019 as a result of their employment. It further asserts that courts are regularly employed as a tool to subjugate media outlets. Among the most regularly used legal instruments to imprison and penalise journalists worldwide are defamation, cybercrime, anti-terrorism, and national security statutes. One of the most prominent examples of this is the case of Maria Ressa, editor of the well-known Philippine news outlet Rappler. Ressa was retroactively tried and found guilty of a "cyberlibel" offence in June 2020 for a study in 2012 on an alleged corrupt relationship between a businessman and a high-ranking judge (Ratcliffe, 2020).

Other types of judicial harassment have been used against journalists by governments and wealthy individuals to trap defendants in protracted and costly legal proceedings and silence any important messages they are trying to report on. These include the use of "SLAPP" lawsuits (strategic lawsuits against public participation), which typically take the form of libel and defamation claims (McGonagle, 2016). While there are numerous instances of laws being used to stifle free speech and target journalists, there are very few instances of legislation that defends journalists and fosters an environment that is supportive of their job. UNESCO (2019) report found that 90% of murderers of journalists go unpunished globally. Attacks on journalists who receive no justice have a chilling impact that extends beyond the particular case. Due to a weakened judiciary, a lack of political courage to take on big entities, or the state itself, or both, many judicial systems are hesitant to act, or inadequately prepared to prosecute violent offenders. Accountability through the local courts is exceedingly challenging due to the absence of judicial independence.

The use and deployment of new technology, as well as data exploitation and surveillance in digital environments, are all factors that put journalists at risk. Journalists frequently encounter man-in-the-middle assaults, coordinated online defamation campaigns, phishing scams, fake domain attacks, and other forms of online abuse.

Journalism is often the target of surveillance and monitoring due to the widespread use of digital technologies and online data collection. This can involve the targeted use of tools such as social media monitoring, malware, spyware, and facial recognition software. Monitoring and surveillance are often used as a means of intimidating and silencing journalists, stifling speech due to the fear of becoming a victim of such tactics and ultimately leading to self-censorship. The capacity of journalists to report securely and freely is also being undermined by state and government efforts to restrict privacy tools like encryption and anonymity, which give them access to information while avoiding censorship and surveillance.

Due to a global fall in advertising revenue, independent journalism's economic viability has been severely hampered globally. Financial coercion and pressure are employed against journalists in such circumstances, especially given the economic depression brought on by COVID-19. Since the transition to digital has put pressure on many media outlets, state policies like the selective allocation of government advertisements, especially in a situation where these advertisements account for the majority of media houses' revenue, can be used as a tool to exert indirect pressure on journalists. Layoffs at media companies are a direct result of the financial unrest and have a negative influence on journalists' livelihoods and well-being. The proliferation of independent journalism has been severely hindered by digital revolutions and reliance on market forces. Local newspapers and media sources, for instance, are fast dwindling and disappearing in the United States (Pickard, 2020). These developments have not only affected information availability and freedom of speech generally, but they also pose more personal risks to journalists who live in continual fear of losing their employment, being laid off, or having their salary reduced.

Protection and Mitigation Strategies to the Threats

Given that states are often blamed for acts of violence and intimidation against journalists, a global examination of state policies is necessary to provide another level of accountability. International interventions, however, have always had problems with enforcement and come with the baggage of neo-colonial practices that utilise press freedom and human rights as a pretext to further more important foreign policy objectives. Before it can be utilised as a tool to hold states accountable, international intervention, which is frequently spearheaded by nations in the global North, needs to be critically analysed. There is a problem with journalist safety, and historically democratic societies are more at risk. The Council of Europe has raised the alarm on the lack of security that journalists suffer within member states after determining that, in 2017, in 28 out of 47 member states, there was insufficient protection against violence and threats.

The effectiveness and proportionality of using procedures like governmental sanctions should be considered. A developing consensus holds that targeted sanctions, as opposed to general embargos, are an effective weapon to guarantee official accountability for press freedoms. The decision-making process must include representatives from the targeted nation's civil society and press freedom watchdogs in order for targeted sanctions to be successful and context-specific.

The best strategy to ensure state cooperation has been to link demands for press freedom and journalist safety to gains from trade and economic access. A policy like the Generalized System of Preferences plus (GSP+), of the European Union links trade benefits to adherence to human rights standards. This strategy can encourage states to pass laws and reform in exchange for benefits in the economy. In addition to other human rights commitments, promoting free expression and journalist safety as economic imperatives can result in structural modifications and the introduction of safeguards. These privileges must include monitoring and procedures for removal in the event of infractions or violations (Dad & Khan, 2020).

There needs to be improvement in the reporting processes for state activities, especially for certain situations. Although there are review mechanisms within the UN system that examine freedom of expression protections at a systemic level, such as the Universal Periodic Review (UPR) process and treaty bodies, the prioritisation of individual reporting of cases involving the targeting of journalists is necessary to ensure accountability. Attacks against journalists are sometimes not reported to or prosecuted by the national legal system, especially when the state is involved. Actors from civil society require assistance to produce thorough reporting on the status of cases.

A concerted and comprehensive policy-making approach to journalist safety is needed, one that involves more than just the conventional international and national stakeholders. It is becoming more and more crucial to take social media businesses' roles into consideration when formulating policies given the significance that online platforms play in the distribution and classification of news items. States in the global South face an even more difficult challenge since they lack the political and financial strength of nations like the United States and European Union members to control social media businesses. However, many policy measures will be insufficient without regulation that mandates social media corporations' transparency and responsibility in relation to content moderation and algorithm use. It is preferable to ensure uniform legal safeguards everywhere through global transparency and accountability for social media corporations' actions than to concentrate responsibility in a small number of more developed nations (Dad & Khan, 2020).

UN Special Rapporteur on the promotion and protection of human rights to freedom of expression called for an embargo on the sale, transfer, and use of surveillance technologies in 2019 until appropriate legal frameworks were in place. The UN High Commissioner for Human Rights recently released a report on the impact of new technology on assemblies, particularly nonviolent protests. Suspects, political rivals, and journalists are routinely monitored by states using surveillance technologies. Sales of surveillance technology to countries with poor or nonexistent privacy protections, such as those lacking robust data privacy legislation, should be strictly monitored and regulated.

The journalism profession is facing increased threats and attacks from various entities that jeopardise its ability to serve the public good. The global political and social instability and technological advancements have allowed for more subtle and sophisticated methods to coerce, manipulate, and attack journalists. Often more insidious than extra-legal approaches, such as censorship and direct repression, the dynamic use of reduced media and information independence, pressure from owners and advertising, and the shifting of professional boundaries has led to an environment where the 'watchdog' role of journalists and the flow of information is constrained. The global nature of these attacks means that all journalists are affected to some degree (YeonLee & Park, 2024). These threats are not exclusive to one type of journalism. Environmental, photojournalism, war correspondents, and foreign correspondents have all faced their own unique hazards in carrying out their work and maintaining their independence.

While journalism remains a vital component of a democratic society, providing the public with information and holding powerful entities accountable, it faces numerous threats that can compromise its integrity and effectiveness, including:

- *Misinformation and Disinformation:* The spread of false, or misleading information, especially through social media and other digital platforms, undermines the credibility of journalism. It can lead to confusion, distrust, and polarisation, making it difficult for legitimate journalism to stand out.

- *Political pressure and censorship:* Governments and political entities may impose restrictions on journalists, leading to censorship, or self-censorship. In some cases, journalists face legal threats, imprisonment, or violence for reporting on sensitive topics.

- *Decline in traditional revenue models:* The shift from print to digital media has significantly impacted the traditional revenue streams for journalism. Advertising revenue has decreased, leading to budget cuts, downsizing, and the closure of news organisations, reducing the resources available for investigative journalism

- *Ownership concentration and media conglomerates:* When media ownership is concentrated in the hands of a few large corporations, it can lead to conflict of interest, reduced diversity of viewpoints, and a focus on profitability over public interest. This can also result in reduced editorial independence.

- *Physical safety and violence against journalists:* Journalists often face threats, harassment, and violence, especially when covering conflict zones, political corruption, or organised crime. These risks can lead to self-censorship, or discourage individuals from pursuing journalism as a career.

- *Digital surveillance and privacy concerns:* The use of digital surveillance by governments and other entities can compromise journalists' sources and their ability to conduct investigations confidentially. This poses a significant threat to the freedom of the press and the safety of sources.

- *Erosion of trust in media:* A general decline in trust toward media organisations can diminish the impact of journalism. Factors contributing to this erosion include perceived bias, sensationalism, and the blending of news with entertainment, or opinion.

- *Technological disruption and automation:* The rise of artificial intelligence and automated content generation can disrupt traditional journalism roles. While technology can be a valuable tool, it can also lead to the spread of low-quality, or misleading content, reducing the need for human journalists (YeonLee & Park, 2024).

Therefore, addressing these threats requires a multifaceted approach involving government regulations, industry reforms, public education, and support for journalistic independence and safety. Collaboration among journalists, media organisations, and civil society is crucial to ensure that journalism continues to serve its fundamental role in society.

Chapter Eleven
Summary of the Book

Chapter one of this book traced the historical antecedent of mass media in Nigeria. The authors established that the historical development of mass media in Nigeria is rooted in the country's colonial history, and its evolving socio-political landscape. Before the advent of modern mass media, Nigeria relied on oral communication. Town criers, traditional leaders, and storytellers served as the primary sources of information dissemination. Instruments such as drums, gongs, and horns were also used for communication within communities. The first formal medium of mass communication in Nigeria was print media, introduced by Christian missionaries in the mid-nineteenth century. The focus was largely on religious, and educational materials. *Iwe Irohin* (1859), founded by Reverend Henry Townsend in Abeokuta, is regarded as Nigeria's first newspaper. It was published in Yoruba, and English, and aimed to promote literacy and disseminate Christian values. Other notable publications followed, including *The Lagos Times* (1880), *The Nigerian Chronicle* (1908), and *The Daily Times* (1926).

By the early twentieth century, Nigerian-owned newspapers like *The West African Pilot* (founded by Nnamdi Azikiwe in 1937) began advocating for independence, and social justice. These publications became platforms for anti-colonial sentiments, providing a voice for emerging Nigerian elites, and nationalists. The introduction of radio broadcasting began with the establishment of the Nigerian Broadcasting Service (NBS) in 1933. Initially, it was a relay station for the BBC but later began local programming. In 1956, the NBS transitioned to the Nigerian Broadcasting Corporation (NBC), marking the first significant step toward locally controlled broadcasting. Following Nigeria's independence in 1960, the mass media diversified and expanded. Government-owned radio and television stations began to emerge. The Western Nigeria Television Service (WNTV) was however established just before independence in 1959 and was the first in Africa. The 1970s, and 1980s saw the proliferation of both state-owned, and privately-owned media outlets, including the rise of tabloid journalism.

The deregulation of broadcasting in the 1990s allowed for the emergence of private radi and television stations, such as *Raypower FM,* and *Channels TV.* The advent of the internet, and digital media in the late twentieth, and early twenty-first centuries have revolutionised Nigeria's mass media landscape, with social media becoming a dominant force. The authors articulated that the development of mass media in Nigeria reflects the country's history, from colonialism to nationalism, and the shift toward democratisation, and globalisation. The mass media continues to play a pivotal role in shaping public opinion, governance, and socio-economic development. The chapter looked at issues like the mass media, classification and types of mass media, historical development of the print media in Nigeria, electronic media discourse, the internet, the internet in Nigeria, social media in Nigeria, types of social media, uses of social media in Nigeria, challenges of social media, characteristics of internet and social media, factors that influence the development of mass media in Nigeria, the combat press of the Nigerian civil war, and boom in government and private press.

Chapter two covered perspectives on journalism and Nigerian women, which are shaped by the interplay of cultural, historical, and socio-economic factors. Women in Nigerian journalism have faced challenges yet made significant strides, contributing to the media landscape in unique ways. The idea of writing, or reporting on important stories, or events with social significance echoes in the discussion of journalism. There are fundamental guidelines for selecting news in journalism because not every writing can be classified as journalistic writing or reporting. A story can be selected for publishing as a news article once all the conditions are satisfied. Journalism includes the task of gathering, evaluating, creating, and presenting news, and information. It is essentially the outcome of these efforts. Journalism is distinguished from other endeavours by certain traits and methods. Since more news and information tend to circulate in countries that uphold democratic values, these factors not only distinguish journalism from other communication mediums, but also provide it significance, and relevance in democratic cultures.

In the second Chapter, the writers demonstrated that the journalists' work is essential to the smooth functioning of society. They consist of, among other things: The term "information function" refers to the collection, and distribution of data regarding events occurring both within, and beyond society. To provide instruction: The ability of the reporter to craft messages that aim to change behaviour, teach knowledge, and clarify procedures is described in this function. To amuse: Statements made public or broadcast with the intention of soothing listeners and lowering their level of anxiety. These duties are completed by the reporter's creativity as they look for noteworthy, and unreported incidents. In this context, the factors that determine news selection in journalism were examined alongside other elements that affect news selection as well as the basic principles of journalism.

It was noted in the chapter that despite the vast array of professional skills, the ideal goal of journalism is to sufficiently inform the target audience about local, subject concerns. Journalism not only keeps the public informed about important facts, and events, but it also provides a forum for competing viewpoints, safeguards government, institutions, and the public, advocates for change that is in the public interest, and constantly seeks the truth. A successful journalist, regardless of career path, needs to be able to write well, handle a heavy workload under pressure, have job experience, possess a range of skills, and above all have a nose for news.

The Chapter re-emphasises that women in Nigerian journalism have been underrepresented, reflecting broader gender disparities in society. In the twentieth century, pioneering women such as Vera Ifudu, Doyin Abiola, Ngozi Anyaegbunam, Chris Anyawu, Onyeka Onwenu, Kadaria Ahmed carved paths in the media. They used journalism to advocate for women's rights, education, and national development. The trajectory point in the chapter is that women journalists often face barriers to entry, and career progression due to cultural stereotypes, and workplace biases. There is a persistent glass ceiling, with women underrepresented in editorial, and leadership positions despite their growing presence in journalism schools, and media organisations. Thus, the profile of Nigerian women in journalism is evolving. Women are challenging traditional norms, influencing media narratives, and advocating for greater representation. However, achieving gender equity in journalism requires sustained efforts to address structural inequalities and cultural biases. The chapter also examined factors that determine news selection in journalism, other elements that affect news selection, the basic principles of journalism, gendered journalism, and factors fuelling gender discrimination in Nigerian news media as well as common hindrances encountered by Nigerian women journalists.

Watchdog journalism in Nigeria broadcast media was discussed in Chapter Three. The authors noted that watchdog journalism connotes the practice of holding those in power accountable through investigative reporting, exposing corruption, abuse, and social injustice. In Nigeria's broadcast media, watchdog journalism has played a pivotal role while facing unique challenges. During colonial times, broadcast media in Nigeria began as a government-controlled entity. The Nigerian Broadcasting Corporation (NBC), established in 1956, largely supported government propaganda rather than independent journalism. Post-independence, the role of broadcast media evolved, but government influence remained significant, particularly during military regimes when censorship was common.

Nigerian broadcast journalists have exposed corruption and human rights abuses. Programmes like "Focus Nigeria" on Africa Independent Television (AIT) and "Sunrise Daily" and "Politics Today" on Channels Television, and "The Morning Show" on Arise Television, have tackled pressing societal issues. Watchdog journalism in Nigeria's broadcast media has drawn attention to inefficiencies in public services, such as healthcare, education, and infrastructure. By scrutinising political processes, and elections, broadcasters help ensure transparency and fairness. The authors argued that many broadcast stations are owned or influenced by political figures, which compromises editorial independence. Government agencies, such as the National Broadcasting Commission, have been accused of using licensing, and fines to stifle dissenting voices. As such, watchdog journalism in Nigeria's broadcast media is vital for accountability, and democracy. While challenges persist, the resilience of Nigerian journalists and the increasing influence of digital platforms provide hope for a stronger, more impactful watchdog role in the future. The Chapter highlighted issues relating to the media as watchdog, Nigerian media, and the watchdog function.

Chapter Four interrogates the concept of investigative journalism, which according to the Chapter is a form of journalism that involves in-depth, detailed reporting to uncover hidden facts, often related to corruption, crime, abuse of power, or other significant societal issues. Unlike routine reporting, investigative journalism requires substantial research, time, and resources to expose wrongdoing, or bring overlooked issues to light. Investigative reporting should first unearth fresh information about a single subject, or concern. An inquiry ought to be unique and provide the audience something new. It should provide "clear, direct, and indisputable proof with no hint of ambiguity," going beyond simple fact-checking.

Investigative journalism in Nigeria has roots in the print media, with pioneers like Nnamdi Azikiwe, and Dele Giwa, who used journalism as a tool for social change. *The Newswatch Magazine,* co-founded by Dele Giwa in the 1980s, was one of the first platforms to consistently produce investigative reports. Other publications like *Tell,* The News magazine, and *Tempo* magazine played major roles in this regard. Digital platforms such as *Premium Times, Sahara Reporters,* and *The Cable* have taken the lead in investigative journalism, uncovering major scandals. Traditional media like *Channels TV* and *Punch Newspaper* also invest in investigative reporting. Investigative journalism is essential for democracy, and societal progress, particularly in Nigeria, where corruption and systemic issues persist. Despite challenges, the courage, and resourcefulness of Nigerian investigative journalists continue to expose injustices and inspire change. With greater support, this field can thrive and further empower the public.

The chapter also discussed the functions of investigative journalism, the traits of an investigative reporter, challenges to investigative journalism, and the future of investigative journalism, where the authors established that investigative reporting has experienced a notable decline in traditional newsrooms, and a rise in internet platforms. The internet has taken over the role of the media in setting agendas and censoring content. With corruption still a major malaise and the state less able to combat it, investigative journalism's normative functions are upheld. Its impact, and the expanded audience reach ensure this. Cooperation, content sharing, and internet usage must all be improved to the degree that investigative journalists see it necessary.

It is important to remember that each story has a different approach; some may require multiple reporters, while others may not. While some stories may be completed within a few days, or weeks, others may require more time to develop into a credible report. This basic understanding will help the reporter decide on the best approach for the story. It would help him develop the positive outlook necessary for the story's good resolution. While some journalists are impatient and unmotivated, others will go above, and beyond to finish an assignment. The theme issues in the Chapter include: the concept of investigative journalism, functions of investigative journalism, traits of an investigative reporter, the difference between conventional and investigative journalism, challenges to investigative journalism, the future of investigative journalism and steps to investigative journalism.

Chapter Five is on political journalism and reporting. It was articulated that political journalism and reporting involve covering events, issues, policies, and figures in politics, often with the aim of informing the public about government actions, political parties, elections, and the broader political landscape. Journalists report on daily developments in politics, including speeches, debates, laws, and policies. This involves gathering information from various sources, including politicians, analysts, experts, and official documents. Political reporters focus on election campaigns, candidate platforms, voter behaviour, and election results. They also analyse political trends, polling data, and the impact of electoral outcomes on future policy decisions. Some political journalists go beyond just reporting facts, offering analysis, or commentary on political trends, policies, and events. This often involves interpreting data, projecting future political shifts, and explaining the implications of political developments. Political journalism plays a critical role in maintaining democracy, holding politicians accountable, and providing voters with the information needed to make informed decisions.

As the Chapter noted, political journalism is a broad field of journalism that includes coverage of all aspects of politics, and political science, even though the term is typically limited to reporting on civil governments, and political power. The goal of political journalism is to inform the public about the activities, and projects of politicians so that voters can make their own decisions, and participate in local, state, or federal issues that impact them. News media use media logic rather than political logic to independently analyse, and portray political information, and political actors adjust to this media landscape. This is known as political news reporting. Journalists covering political news are supposed to be impartial observers who report on politics without any political biases, or inclinations. Reporters are therefore required to keep thorough notes of any modifications to governmental institutions or political offices, every time the newsroom produces an article regarding a change in politics, or government, and ensure necessary updates to their records. For example, in the event of a cabinet change, they obtain a comprehensive list of the new ministers, and add it to the news desk file, and regularly update the files, and confirm the contacts. Issues like political news reporting, elements of good political reporting, political news reporting in Nigeria. The principles of political reporting were discussed.

Citizen journalism is the main content in Chapter Six. The authors established that citizen journalism is the practice where ordinary individuals, rather than professional journalists, play active roles in collecting, reporting, analysing, and disseminating news, and information. This grassroots form of journalism leverages technology, especially digital platforms, to share stories that might not be covered by mainstream media. Unlike traditional journalism, citizen journalism isn't tied to major media outlets. Individuals operate independently, or through informal networks. phones, and social media, citizen journalists often provide immediate coverage of events, especially in crisis or breaking news situations. Citizen journalists frequently cover topics overlooked by mainstream media, offering insights from marginalized communities or alternative viewpoints. Blogs, social media platforms (e.g., X (Twitter), Instagram, TikTok), and video-sharing sites like YouTube are primary channels for citizen journalists. Anyone with internet access and basic recording tools can participate, making it highly inclusive. For instance, during protests, citizen journalists often document events live, such as the Arab Spring, or the #EndSARS movement in Nigeria. Mainstream media may ignore certain events, regions, or issues due to political, economic, or logistical reasons. Citizen journalism addresses this imbalance.

Citizen journalism and traditional media often intersect. News organisations may rely on content from citizen journalists, especially during breaking news events. However, the two forms of journalism differ in terms of training, resources, and accountability standards. Citizen journalism democratises information, making it accessible, and participatory. While it faces challenges related to credibility and ethical standards, its role in complementing traditional journalism, holding power accountable, and amplifying underrepresented voices is invaluable in today's media landscape. With their widespread use and quick development, information, and communication technologies have given people a way to actively participate in the political processes of their own nations. We are now able to rapidly collect, and distribute information to any location in the world because of the extensive usage of smartphones, computers, and the internet.

Traditional forms of journalism are in danger due to the rapid growth of technology. Traditional producer-to-consumer mass communication has been replaced by user-generated media. The Chapter interrogates the position of scholars on citizen journalism, the emergence of citizen journalism in the world, positive and negative influence of citizen journalism in Nigeria, citizen journalism implication for mainstream journalism, citizen journalism, and election monitoring in Nigeria, the cause of the rise of citizen journalism in Nigeria, criticisms, and critical environment of citizen journalism in Nigeria, and ethical issues of citizen journalism practice in Nigeria.

Chapter Seven examined peace journalism, and conflict management. Within this context, peace journalism is a form of journalism that aims to promote peace, and conflict resolution by focusing on constructive, balanced, and non-inflammatory reporting. Unlike traditional journalism, which may highlight violence, division, and sensationalism, peace journalism seeks to uncover the root causes of conflicts, emphasise solutions, and give voice to all sides involved. Peace journalism is a powerful tool for conflict management. By fostering understanding, highlighting solutions, and prioritising humanity over sensationalism, it can help pave the way for peaceful resolutions, and sustainable development in conflict-prone areas. It was articulated that disagreement, clash, collision, struggle, or contests between two, or more parties are all considered forms of conflict; it can also be understood as a situation in which there are conflicting thoughts, feelings, opinions, or desires; a situation in which making a decision is difficult.

Generally, conflict involves competition, and struggle over things that people, and groups value, whether material or not. The tangible things can include limited resources like money, work, political positions, and promotions in both private, and public institutions; the intangible things might be things like culture, tradition, religion, and language. Thus, the media's roles as the fourth estate and watchdog of the realm are both clear and ambiguous. One of the most hotly debated topics in a multicultural, and multiethnic society is how the media should respond to conflict. It is essential that the media promote friendly relationships between people, and groups with numerous, different, and dynamic cultural identities in any culture where the populace is heterogeneous. In this direction, the Chapter discussed the fundamentals of peace journalism, the ten commandments of peace journalism, the emergence of peace journalism, the characteristics of peace journalism, five principles of peace journalism, the practice of peace journalism in Nigeria, challenges of peace journalism in Nigeria, journalists as perpetrators of conflicts, post-conflict peace-building process, conventional strategies for reporting conflict, lessons from American versus Chinese ways of resolving conflict, and media, and conflict reporting in Nigeria.

In Chapter Eight, conflict reporting in journalism was discussed. The authors noted that Conflict reporting in journalism connotes to the coverage of disputes, wars, crises, and tensions at various levels local, national, or international. It involves conveying accurate, timely, and balanced information to the public while navigating ethical dilemmas, safety risks, and emotional challenges. Conflict reporting is a vital aspect of journalism that demands courage, objectivity, and sensitivity. While it often focuses on exposing the harsh realities of war, it can also pave the way for peace by holding power accountable and ensuring that the voices of those affected are heard. Balancing these responsibilities with safety, and ethical considerations is essential for effective conflict reporting.

Every conflict, regardless of intensity, has the potential to jeopardise the peace within a community, region, nation, or even the entire world. Dealing with conflict requires an understanding of its nature, and character, which calls for choosing the appropriate tactics, and identifying the main concerns. Therefore, the causes, characteristics, and dynamics of conflict need to be considered. Despite the assertion that conflict resolution is only a "minimalist requirement" for the establishment of peace, it is actually a major step in that direction. Attempts at definitions that provide a context for comprehending the phenomenon will arise from a more focused thought on conflict. The Chapter examined conflict, phases of conflicts, triangle, and levels of conflict analysis as well as conflict, and manifest conflict reporting, latent conflict reporting from the Nigeria Niger-Delta crisis.

Chapter nine is on Artificial Intelligence (AI), and Algorithmic Journalism, which according to the authors is the use of automated systems, algorithms, and AI technologies to generate, curate, and distribute news content. These technologies have transformed the journalism landscape by enhancing efficiency, accuracy, and personalisation. The Chapter pointed that AI is transforming journalism by automating processes, enhancing content creation, and personalising news experiences. AI technologies enable news organisations to produce more content at scale, analyse complex datasets, and deliver tailored information to audiences. AI is reshaping journalism, offering unprecedented opportunities for innovation, efficiency, and audience engagement. While challenges such as bias, and ethical concerns persist, the thoughtful integration of AI can complement human expertise, ensuring that journalism continues to serve its democratic purpose in the digital age.

The use of artificial intelligence (AI) in journalism has evolved, and is now more widespread, and has a wider range of applications. The application of AI technologies to simulate human cognition in the analysis, interpretation, and comprehension of complex data is a natural fit for the needs of journalism. Journalism is an area that is subject to an increasing amount of AI activity, which is attributed to the large volume of news data available electronically, and the urgency of real-time online journalism.

Equally, algorithmic journalism has to do with algorithms and automated systems to produce, curate, or distribute news content. This approach leverages structured data and rule-based logic to create news stories, analyse trends, and deliver personalised information to audiences. Algorithmic journalism offers significant advantages in speed, efficiency, and scalability, making it a valuable tool for modern newsrooms. However, its adoption requires careful oversight to address challenges like bias, transparency, and ethical concerns. By combining the strengths of algorithms, and human journalists, the industry can harness the full potential of this technology while upholding journalistic standards. In this contestation, AI, and algorithmic journalism represent a significant shift in how news is produced and consumed. While they offer opportunities for efficiency and innovation, their implementation must be balanced with ethical considerations and human oversight. The role of journalists remains indispensable, ensuring that the values of accuracy, fairness, and empathy persist in the rapidly evolving media landscape. The Chapter examined AI, and algorithmic journalism, discusses areas of application of algorithmic journalism, advantages, and disadvantages of automated content production, and interrogated the challenges, and the future implementation of algorithmic technology.

Chapter Ten investigated global journalistic threats, argued that since intimidation, vilification, and violence against journalists have consequences for freedom of expression, democratic values, and public access to information generally, as well as for the targeted journalists. The chapter discussed the most significant, and recent threats to journalists worldwide, and possible policy recommendations that could be made to ensure their safety, and promote an environment that is supportive of accountability, and free speech protections in order to reduce these threats. Journalism and the media have undergone a catastrophic transformation over the past ten years that has fundamentally changed how news is produced, consumed, and transmitted. The Chapter discussed the mapping threats to journalists in the world, and protection, and mitigation strategies to the threats.

The final Chapter, which is Chapter eleven is a summary chapter that provided a synopsis of the entire chapters in the book. It contains the silent points that were raised in the book.

References

Adaja, A. T. (2012). *Nigeria journalism and professionals: Issue and challenges.* http://wwww.iiste.org/journals/index.php/NMMC/art icle/view/2793

Adomi, E.E. (2005). *Internet development and connectivity in Nigeria. Program,* 39, 257-268. https://doi.org/10.1108/00330330510610591.

Agboola, A. K. (2013). Citizen Journalism: A Catalyst for Social Development, and Transformation in Nigeria. In D. Wilson's (Ed.) Communication and the New Media in Nigeria: Social Engagements, Political Development and Public Discourse. *A Publication of the African Council for Communication Education (ACCE),* Nigeria, 216-229.

Aginam, A. M. (2010). *Media and democratization in Nigeria: State, capital and civil society.* (Doctoral thesis, Simon Fraser University, Burnaby, Canada). Retrieved from http://summit.sfu.ca/system/files/i ritems1/ 11542/etd6409_AAginam.pdf

Akinfeleye, R. (2011). *Essentials of journalism: an introductory text.* Lagos: Malthouse Press Limited.

Akinkuotu, A. (1999). *Tell and the Abacha transition. In the media, transition and Nigeria,* edited by Tunji Oseni. Lagos: Tonen Consult.

Ali, A. (2015). Media ownership and control versus press freedom in a democratic Africa. *Journal of Mass Communication and Journalism,* 5(1), 1-5. https://doi.org/10.4172/2165-7912.1000239.

Ali, W., & Hassoun, M. (2019). Artificial intelligence and automated journalism: Contemporary challenges and new opportunities. *International journal of media, journalism and mass communications,* 5(1), 40-49. https://doi.org/10.20431/2454-9479.0501004.

AlQadi, M. F. H. (2024). The uses of artificial intelligence by communicators in developing media content. *Intent Research Scientific Journal,* 3(2), 73-84.

Al-Shami, A. (2019). Unveiling of matters: The role of investigative journalism in uncovering corruption in the Arab world, in B. Hamada, *Off and online journalism and corruption: International Comparative Analysis* (ed) [Electronic]. IntechOpen. Available: https://www.intechopen.com/online-first/unveiling-of-matters-the-role-of-investigativejournalism-in-uncovering-corruption-in-the-arab-world. https://doi.org/10.5772/intechopen.86418.

Alson, J. N., & Misagal, L. V. (2016). Smart phones usage among college students. *IMPACT: International Journal of Research in Engineering & Technology (IMPACT: IJRET),* 4(3), 63-70.

Amodu, L. O., Yartey, D., Ekanem, T., Oresanya, T., & Afolabi, O. (2016, May, 9-11). Assessing the media's watchdog role in ensuring the accountability of the Nigerian government. *Paper presented at the third international conference on African Developmental Issues,* Covenant University, Ota, Nigeria. Retrieved from http://eprints.covenantuniversity.edu.ng/id/eprint/8214

Anyanwu, C. (2001). In Nigerian newspapers, women are seen, not heard. *Nieman Reports,* 55(4), 68-71.

Aondover, E. M., Onyejelem, T. E., & Garba, S. (2024). Media Role in Conflict Resolution and Peaceful Coexistence in Indigenous Communities. *Journal of African Conflicts and Peace Studies*, 6(1), 2.

Aondover, E.M. & Pate, H. (2021). National interest, freedom of expression and the nigerian press in contemporary democratic context. *Brazilian Journal of African Studies*, 6(11), 233-249. https://doi.org/10.22456/2448-3923.103490

Aondover, E.M. & Pate, H. (2021). National interest, freedom of expression and the nigerian press in contemporary democratic context. *Brazilian Journal of African Studies*, 6(11), 233-249. https://doi.org/10.22456/2448-3923.103490

Aondover, E.M. (2017). Peace journalism practice and development in the northeast of Nigeria: Focus Group Discussion with some members of ntal correspondents' Damaturu, Yobe State. *Brazilian Journal of African Studies*, 2(4), 210-226. https://doi.org/10.22456/2448-3923.78201.

Aondover, E.M. (2019). Good governance and accountability: an assessment of the media's role in achieving transparency in the 2019 general elections in Nigeria. *Brazilian Journal of African Studies*, 4(7), 209-225. https://doi.org/10.22456/2448-3923.91505.

Aondover, E.M. Maradun, L. U. & Namadi, H. M. (2021). *Media law and ethics in Nigeria: issues, principles and practices.* Zaria: Ahmadu Bello University Press Limited

Aondover, E.M., & Abba, A. A. (2017). *Understanding Safety and Protection in Nigeria's Journalism.* Ahmadu Bello University Press.

Aondover, E.M., Hile, M. M. Babale, A. M. (2022). *New approach to mass media writing. Zaria.* Ahmadu Bello University Press Limited.

Apata, K., & Ogunwuyi, O. (2019). Media social responsibility and the problematics of investigative journalism among media professionals in OsunState, Nigeria. *Journal of Mass Communication and Information Technology*, 5(3), 1-22.

Apejoye, A. (2024). Contemporary Critiques of Nigerian Journalism. In *The Routledge Companion to Journalism in the Global South* (pp. 251-259). Routledge. https://doi.org/10.4324/9781003298144-26.

Arregui, O. C., & Cheruiyot, D. (2023). The risks of peace: Exploring the relationship between peaceocracy and journalism in Kenya. *International Communication Gazette*, 85(8), 663-677. https://doi.org/10.1177/17480485231214365.

Asemah, E, S. & Ekerikevwe, E. (2013). *Basics of Investigative and Interpretative Journalism.* Jos: Jos University Press.

Asemah, E. (2011). *Selected mass media themes.* Jos: Matkol Press.

Atton, C. (2009). Alternative and citizen journalism. In Jorgensen and Hanitze, T. (Ed.). *The Hand Book of Journalism Studies*, 265-278. Rutledge New York

Banda, F. (2010). *Citizen journalism & democracy in Africa: An exploratory study. Cape town*, South Africa: Highway Africa.

Baran, S. J. (2004). *Introduction to mass communication media literacy and culture* (3rd ed.). New York: McGraw Hill Companies, Inc.

Bassil, C. (2014). The effect of terrorism on tourism demand in the middle east, peace economics, peace science, and public policy, *De Gruyter*, 20(4), 1-16. https://doi.org/10.1515/peps-2014-0032.

Bdoor, S. Y., & Habes, M. (2024). Use Chat GPT in Media Content Production Digital Newsrooms Perspective. In *Artificial Intelligence in Education: The Power and Dangers of ChatGPT in the Classroom* (pp. 545-561). Cham: Springer Nature Switzerland. https://doi.org/10.1007/978-3-031-52280-2_34.

Bender, T. K. (2000). "Imagological considerations in Conrad's vision of Africa" Review of "King Leopold's Ghost" by Adam Hochschild (Book Review). *Clio*, 29(4), 441

Borins, S., & Herst, B. (2019). Beyond "Woodstein": Narratives of investigative journalism. *Journalism Practice*, 2(3), 1-23.

Bortolotto, C. (2024). The embarrassment of heritage alienability: affective choices and cultural intimacy in the UNESCO lifeworld. *Current Anthropology*, 65(1), 100-122. https://doi.org/10.1086/728686.

Brown, N. J., & Udomisor, I. W. (2015). Evaluation of Political News Reportage in Nigeria's Vanguard and The Guardian Newspapers. *Advances in Journalism and Communication*, 3, 10-18. http://dx.doi.org/10.4236/ajc.2015.31002.

Burgh, H. (2008). *Investigative Journalism*, Routledge. https://doi.org/10.4135/9781412964005.n67.

Camaj, L. (2016). Between a rock and a hard place: Consequences of media clientelism for journalist–politician power relationships in the Western Balkans. *Global Media and Communication*, 12(3), 229-246. https://doi.org/10.1177/1742766516675649.

Cheng. L., Kuisin, K. & Li, J. (2008). A discursive approach to legal texts: Court judgements as an example. *The Asian ESP Journal*, 4(1), pp. 14-28.

Chiakaan, G. Oso, L. Egbulefu, C. & Idi, S. (2023). History of the Nigerian media. *Fundamentals of Communication and Media Studies*. National Universities Commission, Abuja, 492-505

Chiakaan, G.J. (2020). *Broadcasting and Broad cast media in Nigeria*. Ibadan: Eagle Prints.

Chocarro, S. (2019). *The safety of women journalists: Breaking the cycle of silence and violence*. Copenhagen: International Media Support (IMS) Book Series.

Chukwu, J. O. (2018). The press and freedom of information in Nigeria and the United States of America: An analysis. *International Journal of Law and Society*, 1(1), 24-33. https://doi.org/10.11648/j.ijls.20180101.14.

Ciboh, R. (2006). *Mass media in Nigeria: Perspectives on growth and development*. Makurdi: Aboki Publishers.

Cohen, B. (1963). *The press and foreign policy*. Princeton: University press.

Coronel, S. (2010). *Corruption and the watchdog role of the news media*. In Norris, P. (Eds), Public Sentinel: News Media and Governance reform, (111-136). Washington, DC, USA: World Bank.

Dad, N., & Khan, S. (2020). *Global conference for media freedom*: Threats against journalists.

Dare, S. (2010). *The rise of citizen journalism in Nigeria* – A case study of Sahara Reporters. http://reutersinstitute.politics.ox.ac.uk/about/article/the-riseofcitizen-journalism-innigeria.html.

De-Clercq, M. (2002). Shedding light on absence: Women's underrepresentation in the newsroom. In *Proceedings of the 23rd conference and general assembly of the IAMCR*, July 21-26, 2002, Barcelona, Spain.

Demarest, L., & Langer, A. (2021). Peace journalism on a shoestring? Conflict reporting in Nigeria's national news media. *Journalism*, 22(3), 671-688. https://doi.org/10.1177/1464884918797611.

Derek, F. (2005). A watchdogs guide to investigative reporting. *Konrad Adenauer Stiftung Media Programme*, 2005, p 4.

Deuze, M. (2003). The web and its journalisms: considering the consequences of different types of news media online. *New Media and Society*, 5(2), 203- 230. https://doi.org/10.1177/1461444803005002004.

Deuze, M., & Witschge, T. (2018). Beyond journalism: Theorizing the transformation of journalism. *Journal of Journalism* 1(9), 165–81. https://doi.org/10.1177/1464884916688550.

Dominick, J.R. (2005). *The dynamics of mass communication.* New York: Harper and Row.

Echeruo, M.J.C (1976*). The Story of the Daily Times, 1926-1976,* Lagos, Daily Times.

Educause Learning Initiative (2007). *7 things you need to know about citizen journalism.* www.educause.edu/eli

Egwu, S. (2013). No boundary between religions, ethnicity in security, safety, welfare, fears, hopes. *Vanguard newspaper*, Thursday 10, 2013.

Ekeli, O. E., & Enobakhare, U. J. (2013). Social media and the changing nature of journalism practice in Nigeria. In D. Wilson, (Ed.), *Communication and the new media in Nigeria* (121-127). Lagos: ACCE Nigeria Chapter.

Ekhareafo, D. O., Okoro., F. E. & Olley, W. O. (2016). *Investigative and interpretative journalism: An insight into critical and review writing.* Trust Publications Lagos, Nigeria.

Emenyeonu, N. B. (1991). Motivations for choice of course and career preferences of Nigerian female students: Implications for the status of media women in a developing nation. *African Media Review*, 5(2), 71-82.

Endong, F. P. (2017). Watchdogging versus adversarial journalism by state owned media: The Nigerian and Cameroonian experience. *International Journal of English, Literature and Social Sciences*, 2(2), 8-17.

Esan, O. (2023). History of film and home video in Nigeria. *Fundamentals of Communication and Media Studies. National Universities Commission*, Abuja, 577-599.

Ezeibe, C. C., & Nwagwu, E. J. (2009). Media imperialism and Crisis of Development. *International Journal of Communication*, 1(4), 65-66.

Fletcher, R., & Park, S. (2017). The impact of trust in the news media on online news consumption and participation. *Digital Journalism*, 5(10), 1281-1299. https://doi.org/10.1080/21670811.2017.1279979.

Freedom of Information Act, (2011). *Laws of the federation of Nigeria.* Abuja: Federal Government Printer.

Gaitano, N. G., López-Escobar, E., & Martín Algarra, M. (2022). *Walter Lippmann's Public Opinion revisited. Church, Communication and Culture*, 7(1), 264–273. https://doi.org/10.1080/23753234.2022.2042344

Galtung, J. (1996). *Peace by peaceful means: peace and conflict, development and civilization.* International Peace Research Institute. Oslo: Thousand Oaks. https://doi.org/10.4135/9781446221631.

Galtung, J. (2000). *The task of peace journalism*: Ethical perspectives. University of Troso, Norway. https://doi.org/10.2143/EP.7.2.503802.

Garba, S., & Aondover, E.M. (2023). Beyond the framing process: An X-ray of newspaper reportage of conflicts in Northern Nigeria. *Unisia*, 41(2), 1-15. https://doi.org/10.20885/unisia.vol41.iss2.art4.

Gearing, A. (2014). Investigative journalism in a socially networked world. *Pacific Journalism Review*, 20(1), 61-65. https://doi.org/10.24135/pjr.v20i1.187.

Ghasemi, A., Farajzadeh, F., Heavey, C., Fowler, J., & Papadopoulos, C. T. (2024). Simulation optimization applied to production scheduling in the era of industry 4.0: A review and future roadmap. *Journal of Industrial Information Integration*, 100599. https://doi.org/10.1016/j.jii.2024.100599.

Godwin, O., Regina, A., & Felix, U. (2019). Assessment of citizen journalism status in Nigeria. *International Journal for Innovative Research in Multidisciplinary Field*, 5(1), 2455-0620.

Gómez-García, S., & Hera, T. (2023). Games as Political Actors in Digital Journalism. *Media and Communication*, 11(2), 278-290. https://doi.org/10.17645/mac.v11i2.6515.

Greer, J. D., & Mensing, D. (2016). The evolution of online newspapers: A longitudinal content analysis, 1997-2003. In L. Xigen (Ed.), *Internet Newspapers: The Making of a Mainstream Medium*. London: Lawrence Associates Publishers.

Hamilton, J. T., & Turner, F. (2009). Accountability through Algorithm. *Center for Advanced Study in the Behavioral Sciences Summer Workshop*. Available online: http://web.stanford.edu/fturner/Hamilton%20Turner%20Acc%20by%20Alg%20Final. pdf

Harber, A. (2020). *So, for the record: Behind the headlines in an era of state capture*. Cape Town: Jonathan Ball Publishers.

Hassan, J. T., Baba, D., Ibrahim, A. A., & Elisha, J. D. (2024). Journalism and social-political conflict in contemporary society. *Journal of Language, Literature, Social and Cultural Studies*, 2(1), 46-58. https://doi.org/10.58881/jllscs.v2i1.151.

Hassan, S. (2013). *Mass communication principles and concepts*. New Delhi: CBS Publishers and distributors Pvt Ltd.

Heaton, M. M. (2024). History of Nigeria. In *Oxford Research Encyclopedia of African History*. https://doi.org/10.1093/acrefore/9780190277734.013.1349.

Houston, B. (2010). The future of investigative journalism. *American Academy of Arts and Sciences*, 1(2), 45-56. https://doi.org/10.1162/daed.2010.139.2.45.

Howard, R. (2002). *An operational framework for media and peace-building*. IMPACS Vancouver, P17.

Idowu, L. (1999). *The Media under Abubakar. In the media, transition and Nigeria*, edited by Tunji Oseni. Lagos: Tonen Consult.

International Press Centre (IPC), (2023). Library. https://www.ipcng.org/

Ishaku, J. (2021). Peace journalism or war journalism? An analysis of newspaper coverage of ethno-religious conflicts in Southern Kaduna, Nigeria (2020-2021). *International Journal of Communication Research*, 11(4), 295-313.

Ismail, A., Khairie Ahmad, M. & Mustaffa, C.S. (2017). Investigative journalism in Malaysia: The battle between outside and inside newsroom challenges. *SHS Web of Conferences*, 3(3), 1- 5. https:// doi.org/10.1051/ shsconf/20173300079.

Jayakumar, K. (2014). *Peace Journalism and Boko Haram*. https://www. insightonconflict.org/blog/2014/06/peace-journalism-boko-haram/

Kaplan, A.D. (2008). *Investigating the investigators: Examining the attitudes, perceptions, and experiences of investigative journalists in the internet age*. Published doctoral dissertation. College Park: University of Maryland.

Kaplan, D. (2020). *What is Investigative Journalism?* https://www.youtube.com/ watch?v=TCVU

Karppinen, K., & Moe, H. (2016). What we talk about when we talk about "media independence". *Javnost - The Public*, 23(2), 105-119. https:// doi.org/10.1080/13183222.2016.1162986.

Klein, D., & Wueller, J. (2017). Fake news: A legal perspective. *Journal of Internet Law*, 20(10), 5-13.

Kuhn, R., & Neveu, E., (eds), (2002). *Political Journalism: New Challenges, New Practices*, London: Routledge. https://doi.org/10.4324/9780203167564.

Kuhn, R., & Nielsen, R. K. (2014). *Political Journalism in Transition: Western Europe in a Comparative Perspective*. London: I.B. Tauris& Co. Ltd. https://doi.org/10.5040/9780755694723.

Kunia, S. S., & Othman, S. S. (2019). Investigative reporting pattern of tempo weekly news magazine. *Humanities and Social Science Reviews*, 7(1), 19-30. https://doi.org/10.18510/hssr.2019.713

Kurfi, M. Y, Aondover, E.M. & Mohammed. I. (2021). Digital Images on Social Media and Proliferation of Fake News on Covid-19 in Kano, Nigeria. *Galactica Media: Journal of Media Studies*, 1(1), 103-124. Doi: https://doi.org/10.46539/ gmd.v3i1.111.

Lanosga, G., & Houston, B. (2017). Spotlight: Journalists assess investigative reporting and its status in society. *Journalism Practice*, 11(9), 1101-1120. https://doi.org/10.1080/17512786.2016.1228472.

Lei, L., Wang, D., Li, T., Knox, D., & Padmanabhan, B. (2011). Scene: A scalable two-stage personalized news recommendation system. Paper presented at the 34th International *ACM SIGIR Conference on Research and Development in Information Retrieval*, Beijing, China, July 25–29, 125–34. https:// doi.org/10.1145/2009916.2009937.

Li, J., Heap, A. D., Potter, A., & Daniell, J. J. (2011). Application of machine learning methods to spatial interpolation of environmental variables. *Environmental Modelling & Software*, 26(12), 1647-1659. https:// doi.org/10.1016/j.envsoft.2011.07.004.

Lippmann, W. (2017). *Public opinion*. Routledge. https://doi.org/10.4324/ 9781315127736.

Lublinski, J., Spurk, C., Fleury, J.M., Labassi, O., Mbarga, G., Nicolas, M.L. &Rizk, T.A. (2016). Triggering change: How investigative journalists in Sub-Saharan Africa contribute to solving problems in society. *Journalism*, 17(8), 1074-1094. https://doi.org/10.1177/1464884915597159.

Lynch, J., & McGoldrick, A. (2005). *Peace journalism (conflict & peacebuilding)*. London: Howthorn Press.

Malam, N. (2006). Ethno-religious conflicts in Nigeria: Revisiting the role of the media. *FAIS Journal of Humanities*, 1(3) 1-18.

Maweu, J. (2017). "Peace propaganda"? the application of Chomsky's propaganda model to the Daily Nation's coverage of the 2013 Kenyan elections. *Communicatio*, 43(2), 168-186. https://doi.org/ 10.1080/ 02500167. 2017.1319873.

McGoldrick, A. (2005). War journalism and objectivity. *Conflict and Communication Online*, 5(2), 1-7.

McGonagle, T. (2016). *Freedom of expression and defamation*, Council of Europe, 2016. https://book.coe.int/en/human-rights-and-democracy/7072-freedom-of-expression-and-defamation.html.

McQuail, D. (2010). *Mass communication theory: An introduction* (6th Edition). London: Sage.

McQuail, D. (2003). *Media accountability and freedom of publication*; Oxford University Press.

McQuail, D. (Ed.). (2002). *McQuail's reader in mass communication theory*. Sage.

Mesmer, K. R., & Miller, K. C. (2024). Who Teaches About Hostility? Examining Factors for Inclusion in Journalism Curriculum. *Journalism & Mass Communication Educator*, 10776958231225709.

Moemeka, A. A. (1991). *Reporters Handbook*. Lagos: Sey-kar Publishers.

Mojaye, E. M. & Aondover, E.M. (2022). Theoretical perspectives in world information systems: A propositional appraisal of new media-communication imperatives. *Journal of Communication and Media Research*, 14(1), 100-106. https://doi.org/10.1515/omgc-2022-0048.

Mudhai, O. F. (2007). Light at the end of the tunnel: Pushing boundaries in Africa. *Journalism Journal*, 8(5), 536-544. https://doi.org/10.1177/1464884907081048.

Munoriyarwa, A. (2018). Have they got news for us? The decline of investigative reporting in Zimbabwe's print media. Communication: *South African Journal for Communication theory and research*, 44(1), 71-88. https://doi.org/ 10.1080/02500167.2018.1441888

Murdock, G and Golden, P. (2005). *Culture, Communication and Political Economy*, in Curran, J and Gurevitch, M (eds) Mass Media and Society (4th ed). London, Hodder Education, pp. 60-83.

Musandu, P. (2018). *Pressing interests: The agenda and influence of a colonial East African newspaper sector*. McGill-Queen's University Press. https:// doi.org/10.1515/9780773556003.

Mushtaq, R. (2019). Pakistan: Woman journalist killed for not quitting job, *The Coalition for Women in Journalism*, November 26, 2019. https:// womeninjournalism.org/cfwijpress-statements/p

Noll, D. (2000). *Conflict escalation: A five phase model*. [Online]. Available: www.mediate.com/articles/noll2.cfm.

North, L. (2016). The gender of 'soft' and 'hard' news: Female journalists' views on gendered story allocations. *Journalism Studies*, 17(3), 356-373. https:// doi.org/10.1080/1461670X.2014.987551.

Nwabueze, C. (2011). *Reporting, principles, approaches, special beats*. Owerri: Top Shelves Publishers.

Nwabueze, C. (2016). *Magazine and newspaper management and production: An introductory text* (2nd ed.). Owerri: Topselve Publishers.

Nwagbara, O. O., Okon, P. E., Nweke, C. J., & Okugo, U. C. (2018). "The role of radio in creating awareness of climate change among crop farmers in Abia State". Nduñöde: *Calabar -Journal of the Humanities*, 1(4), 1-15.

Oberiri, A. D. (2016). Career considerations in journalism among female mass communication students of Taraba State University. *World Scientific News*, 5(7), 13-22.

Odunlami, D. (2023). History of television in Nigeria. *Fundamentals of Communication and Media Studies*. National Universities Commission, Abuja, 541-552.

Ohaja, E. U. (2005). Skills for effective speech and reporting. *International Journal of Communication*, 2, 231-237.

Ojo, T. (2007). The Nigerian media and the process of democratization. *Journalism*, 8(5), pp. 545-550. https://doi.org/10.1177/1464884907081049.

Ojomo, O.W. (2009). *An assessment of broadcast media's role in the political development of Nigeria.* https://www.researchgate.net/publication/320558795

Okon, P. E. (2021). Historical development of the mass media in Nigeria: from colonial era to the present.

Okunna, C. S. (2005). Women as invisible as ever in Nigeria's news media. *International Journal of Media and Cultural Politics*, 1(l), 1-20. https://doi.org/10.1386/macp.1.1.127/3.

Okunna, C.S & Omenugha, K.A (2013). *Introduction to Mass Communication* (3rd.). Enugu: New Generation Books.

Oladokun, O. & Morah, N.D. (2013). Exploring the Realities and Prospect of YouTube in Nigeria. *Journal of Communication and Media Research*, 5(1), 40-56.

Olaito, Y. (2010). *Social media and Nigeria's market/brands.* May 17, 2010.

Omoera, O. S. (2023). Media, culture and conflict in Africa (MCCA)–an introduction. *Media, culture and conflict in Africa*, x–xviii. Newcastle upon Tyne: Cambridge Scholars Publishing.

Omu, F.I.A. (1978). *Press and politics in Nigeria 1880 – 1937.* London: Longman.

Onwubere, C. H. (2016). Press Reportage of the 2015 Presidential Election Campaigns in Nigeria. *Journal of Communication and Media Research*, 8(2),163-176.

Onyemaobi, K. J. (2018). *The role of the press in emerging democracies: An analysis of newspaper coverage of political violence and corruption in Nigeria* (Doctoral dissertation, University of Leicester).

Onyike, I., Amune, P., &Chiaha, C. (2011). *Miracles of the media* (unpublished paper) University of Nigeria, Nsukka.

Orgeret, K.S. (2016). Introduction. Conflict and post-conflict journalism. In Orgeret, K.S. & Tayeebwa, W. (Eds.). (2016). *Journalism in conflict and post conflict conditions- worldwide perspectives*. Nordicom: University of Gothenburg. Retrieved 15 June 2018 from https:// www.reserachgate.net/publication.

Oso, L. (2012). Press and Politics in Nigeria: On Whose Side? Inaugural Lecture Series, 47th Edition, Lagos State University

Oso, L. (2013). Media and democracy in Nigeria: A critique of the liberal perspective. *New Media and Mass Communication*, 10(1), 13-22.

Oso, Lai (2018). Advertisers' Influence of Media Content Production and Distribution, in Popoola, M and Oboh, G.E (eds) *Political Economy of Media Operations in Nigeria*, Oyo, Ajayi Crowther University, pp. 193 211.

Owens-Ibie, N. (2016). Conflicting communication in the communication of conflict: Chibok and narratives on media representation in *Taking Stock: Nigerian Media and National Challenges*, ACSPN Book Series (I), 69-88. www.acspn.org/index.php/books

Oyedele, O.J., Lasisi, M.I. & Kolawole, R. A. (2018). Analysis of foreign aid-induced investigative journalism practice in Nigeria. *Journal of Management and Social Sciences*, 7(2), 435-452.

Palm, M., & Marimbe, S. (2018). *Women in media: Fighting trolls, norms and the occasional bully*. In *Paving the way for good journalism* (27-31). International Media Support Annual Report.

Pate, U. & Dauda, S. (2017). The media, responsibility and conflict-sensitive reporting in Nigeria. Emerging trends in gender, health and political communication in Nigeria.

Pate, U. (2009). Professionalism in the reporting of diversity and conflict issues in the Nigerian. Department of Mass Communication University of Maiduguri.

Pate, U. (2010). *Practices and challenges of media performance in conflict prone multicultural Nigeria*. In E. Soola, H. Batta & C. Nwabueze (Eds.), communication and Africa's crisis: essays in honour of Prof. Des Wilson. Bonn: VDM Verlag Dr Muller.

Pate, U. A., & Jibril, A. (2024). Insurgency in northeast Nigeria: Are journalists safe to report? *Journalism*. https://doi.org/10.1177/14648849241245203.

Patricia E. C., Samuel O., Oluwafisayo O. A, Ifeoluwa O. A, & Omolayo O. J. (2015). Career considerations in journalism among female mass communication students of Redeemers University. *Research on Humanities and Social Sciences*, 5(14), 1-8.

Peter, A. A. (2014). *History of printing and publishing in Nigeria*. https://www.goodbooksafrica.com/2014/03/history-of-printing-and-publishing-in.html?m=1.

Pickard, V. (2020). *Journalism's market failure is a crisis for democracy*, Harvard Business Review, March 12, 2020. https://hbr.org/2020/03/journalisms-market-failure-is-a-crisisfor-democracy.

Pusapati, T. V. (2024). *Model Women of the Press: Gender, Politics and Women's Professional Journalism*, 1850–1880. Taylor & Francis. https://doi.org/10.4324/9781003164708.

Radschi, C. (2011). Forthcoming. The revolution will be blogged: Cyber activism in Egypt. A PhD Dissertation, American University.

Rahim, A., & Bomona, T. V. (1979). managing organizational conflict: A model for diagnosis and intervention. *Psychological Reports*, 44(3), 1323-1344. https://doi.org/10.2466/pr0.1979.44.3c.1323.

Ratcliffe, R. (2020). Journalist Maria Ressa found guilty of 'cyberlibel' in Philippines, *The Guardian*, June 15, 2020. https://www.theguardian.com/

world/2020/jun/15/ maria-ressarappler-editor-found-guilty-of-cyber-libel-charges-inphilippines.

Reporters Without Borders, RWB (2019). Worldwide Round-up of journalists killed, detained, held hostage, in 2019, updated December 17, 2019. https://rsf.org/en/news/rsf-yearly-roundhistorically-low-number-journalists-killed-2019.

Rodny-Gumede, Y. (2015). An assessment of the public interest and ideas of the public in South Africa and the adoption of Ubuntu journalism. *Journal of Media Ethics*, 30(2), 109-124. https://doi.org/10.1080/23736992.2015.1020379.

Rosenthal, R. (2012). A multi-platform approach to investigative journalism. *Pacific Journalism Review*, 18(1), 17-29. https://doi.org/10.24135/pjr.v18i1.287.

Sackey, R., Asiamah, E. O., & Osei-Mensah, B. (2022). Data Journalism in Africa: A Systematic Review. *Advances in Social Sciences Research Journal*, 9(12), 248-259. https://doi.org/10.14738/assrj.912.13612.

Sadiq, A. Z. (2017). Reporting political issues in the Nigerian newspapers: a content analysis of vanguard and leadership newspapers. A research project submitted to the Department of Mass Communication, Faculty of Communication, Bayero University, Kano, in partial fulfillment of the requirements for the award of Bachelor of Science Degree in Mass Communication.

Saleh, I. (2015). Digging for transparency: How African journalism only scratches the surface of conflict. *Global Media Journal African Edition*, 9(1), 1-10. https://doi.org/10.5789/9-1-187.

Sama, J. D. L. C., & Some, K. (2024). Solving fuzzy nonlinear optimization problems using null set concept. *International Journal of Fuzzy Systems*, 26(2), 674-685. https://doi.org/10.1007/s40815-023-01626-7.

Sambe, J.A. (2008). *Introduction to Mass communication practice in Nigeria*. Makurdi: Aboki Publishers.

Sani, S. (2017). An Appraisal of Legal and Institutional Framework for Broadcasting Industry in Nigeria: A Case Study of National Broadcasting Commission (NBC). Unpublished LLM Dissertation. Department of Public Law, Ahmadu Bellow University, Zaria, Nigeria.

Shardow, M. S., & Asare, B. E. (2016). Media ownership and independence: Implications for democratic governance in the fourth republic of Ghana. *Journal of Pan African Studies*, 9(9), 179-199.

Shinar, D. (eds.). (2007). Peacebuilding Journalism: The state of the art. regener. Retrieved 24 June 2018 from https://books.google.com.na/books?

Smyth, F. (2020). Safety of journalists covering protests: preserving freedom of the press during times of turmoil, UNESCO, https://unesdoc.unesco.org/ark:/48223/pf0000374206.

Suleiman, A. (2015). An exploratory study on the use of blogs and citizens journalism materials as news sources by Kaduna Based television stations. A thesis submitted to the school of postgraduate studies Ahmadu Bello University, Zaria in partial fulfillment of the requirements for the award of Master of Science degree in mass communication.

Tafida, A. (2015). Overview of History, Origin and Development of the Mass Media in Northern Nigeria. *South East Asia Journal of Contemporary Business, Economics and Law*, 8(3), 52-58.

Talabi, F. O. (2011). The Internet and Journalism practice in Nigeria. *Global Journal of Human Social Science*, 11(10), 4-18.

Tandoc, E.C., Ling, R., Westlund, O., Duffy, A., Goh, D., &Wei, L.Z. (2018). Audiences' acts of authentication in the age of fake news: A conceptual framework. *New Media & Society*, 20(8), 2745-2763. https://doi.org/10.1177/1461444817731756.

Tang, S. F. Y., & Kirkbride, P. (2018). Developing conflict management skills in Hong Kong: An analysis of some cross-cultural implications. *Management Learning*, 17(3), 287-301. https://doi.org/10.1177/135050768601700315.

Tijani-Adenle, G. (2019). *Women in Nigerian news media: Status, experiences and structures*, (unpublished doctoral thesis), De Montfort University, Leicester, the United Kingdom.

Tilak, G., & Vidyapeeth, T. M. (2020). Journalism and politics. *Journal of Xidian University*, 14(3), 1001-2400.

Tunstall, J. (2024*). The Westminster lobby correspondents: A sociological study of national political journalism.* Taylor & Francis. https://doi.org/10.4324/9781032708850.

Udomisor, I. W. (2013). Management of radio and television stations in Nigeria". *New Media and Mass Communication*, 1(2), 1-14.

Ufuophu-Biri, E. (2006). *The art of news reporting.* Ibadan: Ibadan University Press.

Ukonu, (2005). Precision Reporting in the New Information Society. *International Journal of communication*, 3(5), 67-78.

Unaegbu, L. N. (2017). Safety Concerns in the Nigerian Media. *The assault on journalism: building knowledge to protect freedom of expression*, 171-184.

UNESCO (2019). UNESCO report says 90% of perpetrators of journalist murders go http://www.unesco.org/new/en/rio20/singleview/news/unesco _90_of_perpetrators_of_murders_of_journ alists_remain/.

Uwakwe, O. (2005). *Media writing and reporting.* Enugu: AfrikaLink Books.

Uwugiaren, I., Okocha, C., Ajimotokan, O., &Orizu, O. (2020). Outrage as NBC fines radio station N5m for hate speech. This Day, August 14, 2020. https://www.thisdaylive.com/index-php/2020/08/14/outrage-as-nbc-fines-radio-station-n5m-for-hatespeech/amp/

Van Dalen, A. (2012). The algorithms behind the headlines: How machine-written news redefines the core skills of human journalists. *Journalism Practice*, 6(3), 648–58. https://doi.org/10.1080/17512786.2012.667268.

Vukasovich, C.A. (2012). *The media is the weapon: The enduring power of Balkan War (mis)governance.* Unpublished Doctor of Philosophy Dissertation. Graduate College of Bowling: Green State University.

Waisbord, S. (2015). Watchdog Journalism. In Mazzoleni, G. (Ed) *The International Encyclopedia of Political Communication* (Ist Ed, pp. 1-5). John Wiley & Sons inc. https://doi.org/10.1002/9781118541555.wbiepc046

Wasserman, H. (2018). *Media, geopolitics, and power: A view from the Global South.* Urbana: University of Illinois Press. https://doi.org/10.5406/j.ctt21c4tj6.

Wasserman, H. (2020). The state of South African media: A space to contest democracy. *Publizistik*, 65(3), 451-465. https://doi.org/10.1007/s11616-020-00594-4.

Westlund, O., Krøvel, R., & Orgeret, K. S. (Eds.). (2024). *Journalism and Safety: An Introduction to the Field.* Taylor & Francis. https://doi.org/10.4324/9781032705750.

Wilson, J. Balka, M. M. & Fredrick, W. (2023). Internet and social media in Nigeria. *Fundamentals of Communication and Media Studies.* National Universities Commission, Abuja, 600-610.

Yahaya, J. (2011). Ethnic and religious conflicts in Kaduna and Plateau states: Implications for development in Nigeria. Online on 23/07/2017.

Yar'Adua, S. M., & Aondover, E.M. (2020). Peace journalism and development: An appraisal of Boko Haram insurgency in the north-east of Nigeria. *International Journal of Health, Safety and Environment (IJHSE)*, 6(7), 608 – 617

Yékú, J. (2022). *Cultural netizenship: Social media, popular culture, and performance in Nigeria.* Indiana University Press. https://doi.org/10.2307/j.ctv2b29sw4.

YeonLee, N., & Park, A. (2024). Unraveling the Digital Threat: Exploring the Impact of Online Harassment on South Korean Journalists' Professional Roles. *Journalism & Mass Communication Quarterly.* https://doi.org/10.1177/10776990231217448.

Yuan, W. (2010). Conflict management among American and Chinese employees in multicultural organisation in China. *Cross Cultural Management*, 17(3), 299-311. https://doi.org/10.1108/13527601011068388.

Yusha'u, M. (2009). Investigative journalism and scandal reporting in the Nigerian press. *Ecquid Novi: African Journalism Studies*, 30(2), 155-174. https://doi.org/10.1080/02560054.2009.9653400.

Zafrullah, Z., Hardi, V. A., Nabilah, N., & Fitriani, A. (2024). Transforming the Utilization of ChatGPT in Education: A Bibliometric Analysis. *Innovative: Journal of Social Science Research*, 4(1), 5610-5623.

Zhong, R., Zhang, E., & Munetomo, M. (2024). Cooperative coevolutionary surrogate ensemble-assisted differential evolution with efficient dual differential grouping for large-scale expensive optimization problems. *Complex & Intelligent Systems*, 10(2), 2129-2149. https://doi.org/10.1007/s40747-023-01262-6.

Index

V

W